DEDICATION

In loving memory of the most amazing man of God I ever knew—a man who loved me unconditionally for forty-five years.

To my children:
Donna, Judy, Shelley, John, Anna

To my fourteen precious grandchildren:
David, Vicki, Zack, Isaac, Adam,
Jessica, Sarah, Matthew, Rachel,
Joey, Diego, Abby, Alex, and Annabelle

To my dear friends—Harold and Teany Ramsey

To our faithful supporting pastors who made it possible to stay in the Battle for Souls in Argentina for nearly thirty years.

ACKNOWLEDGMENTS

I want to thank everyone who encouraged me to write this book and upheld me in pray. I could not have done this without the support of my family, both immediate and extended. I know it was only with the Lord's help that I was able to write it. Thank you my dear friend Teany Ramsey—who was just a phone call away—and who encouraged me so many times when I felt like I couldn't go on. A huge thank you to Reverend Thomas Ray for giving me suggestions on how to start my book and gave me the perfect name for it. Thank you dear friends in our widows' group at Treasure Valley Baptist Church, and to the many other friends and members who prayed daily for me. Thank you to our dear Argentine pastors, their families and churches who have prayed for me and encouraged me. They dearly loved their pastor, and they have been such a blessing to me. And a special thank you to Erika Peterson and my daughter, Shelley, for their advice and for the hours they spent reading and correcting my many writing mistakes, and to my son, John, for his knowledge and wisdom concerning my finances, and to my daughter, Anna, who made sure that I had everything I needed.

I woke up one morning in February of 2010, and the following poem began to form in my mind and heart. I had never written a poem before, but these words just seemed to flow out of my heart.

THE ONE I'VE LOVED

My heart longs to see the face of the one that I have loved,
but he's gone on to Heaven to his Savior up above.
I think of all the things we shared:
The joy, the laughter, the love, God's care,
And I know that Christ will give me grace
To bare this burden till I see his face.

I know the day will come when my joy shall be complete,
when I go to heaven to sit at Jesus' feet.
But for now, I'll trust Him day by day to give me grace
and peace to stay.
I'll serve my Savior faithfully until the day He comes for me.
And as I step through Heaven's door above
I'll see the face of the One I've loved.

PREFACE

THE QUESTION THAT CHANGED OUR LIVES

When Don walked in the door that beautiful spring day, I knew there was something serious going on in his mind and heart. He looked at me and said, *"Hey honey, if the Lord opened the door to go to the mission field, where do you think He would want us to go?"* That was the question and the moment that changed the whole direction of our lives. It was April 1972. Three months later we started our incredible journey in preparation to go to Argentina, South America.

We had just bought a wonderful church property and had moved into the beautiful parsonage. Our first service in the new church was to be Easter Sunday. We were so excited about the property. It had been six and a half years since we had started the Bible Baptist Church of Long Beach, California. We had moved seven times. Don used to laugh and say that if someone missed one Sunday, he or she might never be able to locate us again. The last of the seven moves had been into a church building that we had purchased four years before. It seemed great at the time, but we quickly outgrew the facilities. At last we finally had church facilities where we could actually take care of at least eight hundred people. We were excited and had great plans to move forward, win souls, and fill up this new church building that God had provided for us. Then, to our amazement, God opened the door for us to go to the mission field. We felt that God's plan for us had been to stay in Long Beach, California, but He showed us that He now had a different direction and plan for our lives.

Our hearts had always been in missions. We both majored in missions at Baptist Bible College. Our church supported about twenty-five missionary families all over the world. We loved being with them and hearing about their different fields and the work that they were doing. A few weeks before moving into the new church property, we had our annual mission conference. A missionary couple from Argentina presented their field, and God dealt in Don's heart as well as mine about this field. If the Lord called us to the mission field someday and opened the door for us to go, Don wanted us to go out under the Baptist Bible Fellowship. He really wanted to be sent out by them.

A couple of years after starting our church in Long Beach, we had our first Faith Promise Missions Conference. Don committed to give $15 each week. You must understand that back then that was a huge step of faith, since it was nearly a fourth of our total income. I was a stay-at-home mom, and Don drove a school bus part-time. We were used to living on a very small budget, and the amount seemed incredible to me. But I didn't balk at it since Don knew that it was what the Lord would have us give. God supplied that year by giving us good health. We spent only $25 the entire year on doctors and medicine. The year before, there were times when we were in the doctor's office every day of the week with our sick baby. It was so amazing to watch God supply our needs throughout the following years. From that first mission conference, our hearts were truly in missions. Each time a missionary would come, we would be burdened for their field of service and their needs, but not until the family from Argentina came and presented their field did God so strongly impress upon our hearts and burden us to go. A few weeks later, when God actually opened that door, I was completely amazed that He would call us and allow us to go and be His missionaries on a foreign field. I felt serving as missionaries to be such a privilege then, and still I feel that it was a privilege for us to have been able to go to Argentina to serve the Lord.

As in every aspect of our married life, when God spoke to Don about doing something and then opened the door, he literally ran through it and never looked back. Don's faith in God and his ability to trust Him always amazed me. As a matter of fact, everything about my husband has amazed me. If you would allow me to do so, I would love to tell you about this man who came from a very difficult childhood, became steeped in sin by age twenty-six, and who suffered rejection on many different levels. Through many trials, injuries, illnesses, and unimaginable pain, he just wouldn't quit or give up. Under similar circumstances most men would have just tossed in the towel, so to speak, and said "Enough is enough!"

1

"IF I'D HAD $25 AT THE TIME..."

"IF I'D HAD twenty-five dollars at the time, you never would have been born." Don heard these words over and over as he was growing up. Every time he'd do something to upset his mother, she would throw these terrible words at him. She'd had nine abortions before she became pregnant with Don. He never really knew whether she would have aborted him if she'd had the money at the time, but it's what she told him over and over again. As in Jeremiah, God had His protective hand on this new life even before he came out of the womb.

"Before I formed thee in the belly I knew thee; and before thou camest forth out of the womb I sanctified thee, and I ordained thee a prophet unto the nations." Jeremiah 1:5

Even though she said this time and time again, she was actually very protective of her two little dark Mexican Jewish kids. His sister, Dolores, had been born three years before Don. The kids were the product of an unusual and very rarely accepted union of a Mexican man and a German Jewish woman in the early 1930s. Don's dad came and went from the time his sister was born but left for good when Don was about three years old. He and his sister lived with their mother and Jewish grandparents. His father went to Sonora, Mexico, and married a young, deaf Mexican girl. Don did not see his dad again until he was fifteen years old.

Don, being a very active and mischievous little boy, was always in hot water with his grandfather. Living with older grandparents definitely had its challenging moments. His grandfather was very protective of his tools, and it became a very huge temptation for Don and Dolores to play with them outside in the yard. Problem was, they would forget to put them back. Since Dolores seemed to be the favorite of her grandfather, their mother would tell Don (lovingly called Donnie in those days) to just say that he was responsible, because his grandfather didn't like him anyway. Dolores seemed to always get away with the crime, but it didn't seem to bother Don, because he idolized his big sister. Those two were inseparable during their growing-up years. After he had witnessed to her for forty years, she finally accepted the Lord as her Savior in 2002 after Don had had a massive stroke. In 2006, at the age of seventy-three, Dolores went home to be with the Lord. Don was seventy at the time, but he was still her "baby brother." Don loved to tell us about their escapades.

Don age 10 with Dolores age 13

*Don and Dolores after she received
Christ as her Savior.*

During World War II, they discovered the life of hobos. They decided that would be a fun way to live, so they ran home, raided the kitchen pantry, took their stash, and went down to open the cans and eat them under the railroad bridge where many of the hobos lived. They were really a couple of characters. Don was a carefree little guy who often found himself and his sister in trouble. He remembered that there were nights when he and Dolores would take graham crackers, a flashlight, and a book to bed with them. Thinking that their mother would never catch on to what they were doing, they would read their books, enjoy their graham crackers, and lay there under the covers laughing and talking until very late. However, one night their mom heard them, and when she got up to check on them, she came dashing in, kicked the bed, and broke her big toe. Needless to say, there were two kids in big trouble that night. Many years after we were married, I would hear them tell this same story over and over and always just crack up laughing at each other.

During this same time period, Don's mom would take Dolores and him down to Tijuana. They loved these outings. It was great fun to watch his mom haggle with the merchants. When she finally got them down to the price she wanted, she'd turn around and walk out of the store, saying that she really didn't want it anyway. Don said it was fun watching her when they were young, but as they grew, it began to embarrass them. Funny thing about it is that years later, Don would do the same thing when we were in language school in Mexico. The kids thought it was great, but when we arrived in Argentina, it was a different story. The kids were getting older and at an age to get embarrassed easily. Don would try to get the price down, but they do not play that game in Argentina. The store owner would end up getting upset about it. It took me years to realize that it was Don's Jewish way of thinking. Although he had been a first-rate door-to-door salesman for two different products, he never could sell any of our used things, because he wanted to get enough out of them to actually replace them.

Don's early years were not always fun ones. When Don was about five years old, there was a butcher shop in the neighborhood. He'd go down there and talk to Ace, the butcher, for hours. He'd always ask him for a "wiener," and this cute little kid with the big smile usually got what he wanted. A couple of years later, his mother married the butcher, but there was a problem with this "kind" butcher. He was an alcoholic. He'd get drunk, and Don, his mom, and his sister would have to run away from him. On one of these occasions, they fled to the house across the street where an old couple lived. They were Christians, and years later, after Don was saved, he remembered that they witnessed to his mom that night. She began to read the Bible to them after that, but that lasted only three nights. That was the first time in his young life that he received a witness of Christ; still, in later years, he didn't believe that God really existed.

His stepfather, Ace, began to write bad checks, along with breaking other laws, and ended up in prison. Don's mom would take Dolores and him with her when she went on visitation days. One day while she was visiting Ace, she met her next husband. Don's life was going from one drunken stepdad to another. To watch Don during those years, though, you would have thought he didn't have a care in the world. One of his childhood buddies, Don Crosby, told me that he had no idea what kind of life Don was living, because he always seemed to be such a happy kid and made everyone around him laugh.

During the war, he and his friends stopped playing cowboys and Indians and began playing war games. One of his friends decided that his own dad was a German spy, and they spent many hours spying on him. This man had a shortwave radio, and he spent a lot time listening to it and talking to others, but thankfully, he just proved to be a regular dad very interested in finding out all he could about what was going on in Europe.

Being a busy, industrious, and very patriotic kid, Don wanted to do his share to help with the war. He'd collect scrap metal, glass bottles, and whatever else he could find that could be used in the factories for the war cause. He sold newspapers and bought war bonds with the money. He was chosen to play the part of Uncle Sam in a school program. This was really very unusual—to have a dark-skinned little Mexican boy playing Uncle Sam—but he stood proud and quoted the Gettysburg Address. He was also in the school choir during this period of time. He tried his best to sing the notes, but after a while, his teacher asked him to just move his lips but not let any sound come out. He even tried to take piano lessons but laughingly told us that he never was able to get off the cardboard piano to try a real one.

This lack of musical talent followed him through all his years. When we were first married, we would be standing together singing during the song service. Being a very happy Christian, Don would sing with all his heart. Little kids would turn around and look at him, and he'd just smile and keep on singing. Things like that didn't bother him. After all, he was "making a joyful noise unto the Lord." He received a lot of teasing through the years, especially from his own kids.

2

ALL THE WORLD LOVES A CLOWN

AT AGE TWELVE Don began setting pens at the Boulevard Bowl. This began his fourteen-year-long love affair with bowling. His life at home was extremely miserable, but he now had a place where he could escape to each night. One never had to wonder where he was in the evening: he would either be setting pens or practicing. His mom and Dolores would spend many evenings at the Boulevard Bowl watching Don practice over and over again. His friends began to call him "Kid Mexico." At age fourteen he began to keep scorecards. In a short time, he could keep score for up to six lanes at one time. He made $2.00 a night doing this. It used to fascinate me how he could add up figures so quickly. He told us it was from keeping score on so many lanes at one time. This came in handy in the mission field, where the exchange rate would change two or three times a day. He never had a problem with quickly figuring out what the dollar was worth.

He joined the Poly High Bowling team and soon became a very proficient bowler. His teammates became his best friends, and they spent many, many hours each week together. Their team was California State champs for two years in a row. He was team captain of the Junior LA All-Stars Team Champs. They were a traveling team. Sometimes he'd get caught up telling me about those days, and he'd laugh at some of their antics. One time they played a ladies' league team and beat them. All of the boys were just teens, and these ladies were a champion bowling team. These kids were really hotshot bowlers, and some went on to bowl professionally for many years.

During this same period of time, he began to skip school with some of his friends. In his junior year, he had fifty-two days of truancy. He and his best friend, Billy Maglioni, would go up to Big Bear in the mountains. They'd ski and just hang out.

Things were getting very complicated in Don's life. He was actually very shy and didn't like speaking in front of people. He dropped out of school twice in the tenth grade because he was told to give an oral book report. He began to realize that acting like a clown and making people laugh would help hide what was really going on in his life. He and his mom were always fighting, and his sister was hanging out more and more at the Pike with sailors. The Pike was an amusement zone in Long Beach. For a time Don lived with Billy and his dad. Pop Maglioni liked Don and was happy to have him hanging out with Billy. He taught Don to cook good Italian spaghetti sauce among other Italian dishes. Don and Billy became inseparable buddies and did everything together.

Another good friend of Don's was Don Crosby. Although Crosby was two years older than Don, they bowled together on the high school team and went on to bowl together from 1949 to 1952 and then from 1959 until around 1960. Crosby recently sent me pictures and a lot of information on their bowling teams: scores, different leagues, sponsors, and statistics. Much of this information was new to me but not the names of the bowlers who were Don's friends. He had talked about them a lot during our life together. When Crosby called me after Don passed away, I was so surprised to hear from him, because they had lost contact with each other for many years. He graciously filled me in on a lot of information about that time in their lives. Although Crosby lived only one block away from Don when they were growing up, he never had a clue of the tragic life that this young Mexican kid was living. Crosby said, "There were so many things I didn't know about his mother and his hard life growing up! I don't remember him ever complaining, but I was on the bowling side of his early life…his happy time."

When Don was fifteen, his dad came back to Long Beach to see him. He wanted to take Don on a trip down to Mexico to hunt and fish. It was the first time he had seen his dad since he'd left when Don was three years old. They went down to Sonora, where his dad lived on a peninsula, and went fishing. Then he took Don on a camping trip to go hunting. Don told me he could remember camping out in the open and lying there next to his dad, just looking up at the stars and thinking how safe he felt lying there next to this huge man. He never again had that opportunity.

During several summers of his teen years, Don worked on fishing boats. He'd take care of the bait tanks, getting the poles set up, cleaning up the boat at the end of the day, and many other jobs. He loved it all. Anything and everything about fishing fascinated him.

During this time he was not only introduced to bowling, keeping scorecards, and learning to add quickly, but also to the vices that came along with the bowling crowd of that time. At sixteen he had his first cigarette and his first beer on the same night. This began a whole new cycle in Don's life. He smoked for the next ten years, and by the time he got out of the army, he was an alcoholic. He was a fun kid who made people laugh, and they liked being around him. The more he drank, the more of a clown he became, and the more he would make people laugh. Whenever there was something to do, they would always call him to go along, and he seldom refused the invitation. His response was always: "Sure, put me down, I'll go." He was fast gaining a reputation of "Sure, put me down I'll go Espinosa."

After he dropped out of high school, he traveled a lot with his bowling team. He was quickly becoming addicted to gambling. He and his friends would gamble on anything and everything. In one of his messages, he tells about those days: "I was so addicted to gambling that I would gamble on anything—horse races, dog races, poker, dice, you name it. One time a friend and I were going to San Francisco to play in a big tournament. Do you know what we did to gamble? We'd take a crayon and draw circles on the windshield, and we would bet on who would be the first to get a bug smashed in his circle. We'd see two birds sitting on a fence and bet whose bird would fly away first." Sounds funny, but this was just the beginning to his addiction to gambling. These vices led to some serious consequences later on in his life.

He was seventeen when he dropped out of school and got a job delivering Cadillacs for a dealership in Long Beach. He and a buddy would pick up the car, go eat breakfast, and then deliver it. After a few weeks, the dealer hired some more delivery boys, and

Don thought that he was going to be promoted to a better-paying job. But, instead, he was fired along with his buddy, because the boss had found out about their little time-outs for breakfast. It went this way for a couple of years; he just drifted from one job to another.

In 1951 he was in a bowling slump. The Korean War was going hot and heavy, and young men were being drafted each month. Don was sick of his home life, and Billy had been drafted. Don knew that if he volunteered for the draft, he would get out in two years instead of the usual three. He signed up for the voluntary draft and was called up in April 1951. He was sent to Camp Roberts. Here was a new young Don Espinosa—a gung-ho soldier going to war in Korea.

3

DO IT WITH ALL YOUR MIGHT

ECCLESIASTES 9:10 SAYS: "Whatsoever thy hand findeth to do, do it with thy might; for there is no work, nor device, nor knowledge, nor wisdom, in the grave, whither thou goest." Even as an unsaved young man, Don was determined to train hard and be prepared to have the best chance possible to survive if he was sent

to the front in Korea. He had always been gung-ho about most everything he did, but this was different. This was for survival's sake. He was being sent to Camp Roberts. It was known all over that if you were trained there, you would be immediately sent to the front lines when you got to Korea, because you were highly trained in machine-gun warfare. He just knew in his heart he would be sent to the front lines.

The month he was drafted, there were ninety thousand young men called up for this war, which was going hot and heavy at that time. There had been over fifty-four thousand men killed already. However, when he went in to report, they sent him home with a three-day pass because there were so many drafted that they didn't have room for him on the train to the base.

When Don actually started basic training, he loved it. He not only loved the workouts and artillery training, but he loved the discipline. He had never had a structured life before this. He really loved training with the machine guns, rifles, and bayonets as well as the hand-to-hand combat. These are Don's own words about that training time taken from a message he preached using the text in Ecclesiastes 9:10:

I listened to every word that was said in those training sessions. I wanted to learn everything I could about the equipment I was going to be using. I wanted to hit the bull's eye every time I used the rifle. I remember that we went out to the bayonet assault course. Talk about feeling mean. When I put that bayonet on the end of my rifle, which back then was a M1, I felt like the baddest dude around, and I could see those Koreans hanging onto the end of my bayonet all over the place. So we got out there to this bayonet assault course. We had our bayonets fixed, and we had a grenade that didn't have any dynamite in it, only the fuse. We got up there, and there was a foxhole about twenty yards up this hill. So the cadre said, "Don't throw it into the hole, and it will just roll down to you. If you throw it into the foxhole, you will have to go up after it." I thought, what's this guy talking about? I'm going to show him that I can throw it right into that hole. I pulled the fuse and threw it, and it went right into the hole. Then I went charging up the hill: here comes gung-ho Espinosa. I jumped into the hole, bayoneted that dummy, got my grenade, and ran back down that hill. I jumped into another foxhole, but there was a root sticking up in that hole, and I hit it and sprained my ankle. My leg was in a cast for a month, and the war ended while I was in the hospital healing up. But believe me, I wasn't saved at the time but it was biblical: **"Whatsoever thy hand finded to do, do it with all thy might."**

At another time we were out at the assault course with the bayonet fixed. Those rifles had a wooden stock that was made out of oak. It was one of the hardest woods there was. This time we were to charge up the hill and hit a wooden post with the stock. There again I could picture myself charging toward the enemy standing there, and I was going to knock his head off. I hit that post with everything I had, and I broke the stock off of my rifle. There I stood, a hundred and thirty-two pounds. That's what I weighed. I mean, I hit that thing so hard, and out of a company of 250 men, there were two of us that day that broke the stock off our rifles. And the other guy looked like Hercules, 250 pounds of muscle. They said that if you broke the stock off the rifle, they would give you a three-day pass. Boy, I was so proud. You should have seen me, man, strutting back in with the broken rifle. I had given it everything I had. The company commander looked at it to see if the stock was rotten. He figured for me to have broken it, it must have been rotten, but it wasn't. What I'm trying to tell you is that I did it with all my might.

Instead of being sent to Korea, he was sent to Orleans, France, where he was stationed for two years. Don started out as a truck driver, then became a clerk typist, and then was transferred into the MPs. He was court-marshaled twice: once for being drunk while on duty, and the other time for leaving his post without relief.

One of Don's best buddies was an American Indian named James Loclear. He was also an MP. James was from the Lumbee Indian tribe of North Carolina, who many believe intermarried with the colonists of the mysterious Roanoke colony in Virginia because of their blue eyes. When James entered the army, he claimed to be a Cherokee. He was a mean guy, ready to fight all the time. But he and Don got along great. They'd go out drinking together and get in bar fights, and James was always ready for a good fight. The military police shared their barracks with the cooks. They usually all got along pretty good, but one night one of the cooks made a remark about James's dog tags and his Indian status. After a few heated comments, Don punched the cook, and the fellow fell over the bed. When he got up, Don told him, "OK, now you hit me!" The next thing Don knew, he was hit in the nose and was down for the count! The next day when he and his friend, James, were talking about the evening before, it turned out that James had flattened him! Don said that James had a hand twice the size of his. James had taken him up on the offer to hit him.

While Don was on deputation in 1973, some eighteen years later, he was traveling in North Carolina and stopped in to look up his old friend. He looked in the phone book, but there were several James Loclears in the listings, so he stopped by the local high school. He looked over the yearbooks, but there wasn't one for his friend's year. While he was wondering what he should do next, a fellow asked him if he could help him out. It turned out to be James's brother! The man gave Don his brother's address, so Don went right over to see him. He had every intention of witnessing to his old buddy. When they began talking, Don found out that James had had received Christ just three weeks before Don came. His wife had been saved first, and James had followed after attending church for a few weeks. Don was thrilled to death. That night he and James went visiting in the neighborhood, and while no one received Christ, it was such a blessing to Don to be doing something for the Lord with his former drinking buddy. That night James gave Don $50 dollars for his mission work. He wanted to have a part in the salvation of souls in Argentina.

When Don was discharged from the army, he was a twenty-year-old alcoholic. He got back into bowling and said that his one claim to fame was that he beat pro-bowlers—Bob Strampe, Dick Hover, George Howard, and Don Galenski—playing nine-ball in San Francisco during the Fourth of July tour. Some of these men went on to be well-known in the bowling world. He bowled with his team in the national tour in Rochester, New York, then in Detroit, Michigan. They went from there to Sioux City, Iowa, where he and other members of his team got into a fight and parted ways. In 1996 we were in Saint Louis, Missouri, and went to the Bowling Hall of Fame. As we were leaving, he said, "Praise God, I'm not enshrined there along with many of my old bowling buddies. God saved me and lifted me out of that crowd and changed my life."

Soon after parting ways with his team, he joined the forestry service as a firefighter. He had some pretty entertaining stories to tell about this time. If our kids started feeling sorry for themselves about circumstances that weren't going their way, he'd start in with "you think you have it bad, but were you ever drilled in the leg by a rivet gun?" From there he'd start telling about his adventures in the forestry service and how he was nearly trapped in the middle of a fire, because he had jumped right in there to fight it from the center, but then his hose burnt in half. By the time he'd finish with his tall tales, the kids would be in stitches laughing and would forget all about their problems.

He worked in a logging camp for a while and from there returned back to Long Beach where he was hired on at the Douglas Aircraft factory. At twenty-two he married and soon had a baby girl, Donna. He became a lead man at Douglas and was making $1.48 an hour, which in that day was a good salary. However, there was never enough to live on. He drank and gambled it away. For the next four years, he lived in misery, getting deeper and deeper in sin.

4

"IF THAT'S ALL THERE IS TO IT, I'LL GIVE IT A WHIRL"

THROUGH THE YEARS Don had been exposed to the witness of Christ. The first time, as I mentioned in another chapter, was when he was just a child and running away from a drunken stepdad. Those neighbors, an older couple, were very kind to Don and his mom and sister when they needed a refuge. When Don worked at Douglas Aircraft, there was one of those "religious fanatics." Don would see him reading his Bible during break times and praying over his meals. For a time Don thought that he was just one of those "lily-livered Psalm singers."

Until this time Don had been an atheist. He didn't believe that God existed. When he was in junior college, he had a professor that had an extremely high IQ, and he taught the "big bang" theory. Don figured if this near-genius believed it, it had to be true. Don believed that one was born either a good guy or a bad guy. He felt he'd been born a bad guy, so what difference did it make?

However, this time he had come in contact with a real Christian. In his testimony, written before we were approved as missionaries, he said, "I had met a true Christian. He had what was missing in my life. He told me how Jesus had saved him and given him a new life. Although he didn't actually show me how to be saved, the Lord used him to plant the seed in my heart to desire to have whatever it was that he had. I could see that he had peace in his heart."

There was a parking lot attendant who sometimes parked Don's car. Each time Don returned to pick up his car, this attendant had left the radio on a Christian station. One day Don decided to listen to it to see just what the attendant found so interesting. God was planting the seeds, one at a time, in Don's heart, but by now it had been five years since that Christian at Douglas Aircraft had witnessed to him. His life had spiraled downward through those five years. He was a drunkard, addicted to gambling, and steeped in sin and the things of this world. In giving his testimony one time, he said that he knew in his heart there had to be more to life than the misery he was living in.

There was a Christian couple who bowled with Don. They really didn't go along with all the things that were happening in the bowling alley, but then they never took a stand against it either. You can imagine Don's surprise when they asked him to go to church with them. They explained that he would be doing them a big favor. He could help them win a Bible in the "apple orchard" Sunday school campaign. He'd never been to Sunday school in his life. His dad was Catholic, but he had left by the time Don was three years old, and he had never taken him to the Catholic Church. His mother was Jewish, but after her father had a fight with the rabbi over money, their family had never returned to the synagogue. But true to his reputation, he said, "Sure, put me down, I'll go."

During the week this couple, Bill and Betty, called and asked if they could bring their pastor over to meet him on Friday evening.

Don was really nervous about this but agreed to it. Pastor Meek showed up with Bill and Betty and Mrs. Meek. Pastor Meek began to talk to Don and answer all his questions. Don kept coming up with unimportant things, thinking it would stump this preacher, but Brother Meek kept giving him scripture after scripture to answer those questions and arguments. He took him through the plan of salvation using the "Roman Road*," and after three hours Brother Meek looked at Don and said, "Don, would you like for me to lead you in a word of prayer to ask the Lord to come into your heart and to forgive you of your sins?" Don looked at him and said in his flippant way, "If that's all there is to it, I'll give it a whirl."

Brother Meek led him in a word of prayer, showed him some scriptures on eternal security, and then left with Mrs. Meek and Bill and Betty. As they walked away from the house, Don's friends were really angry. Pastor Meek wasn't too happy either. They really thought that Don was just trying to get rid of them by praying the sinner's prayer. BUT GOD! In His wonderful grace reached down and heard that sinner's prayer and gloriously saved this young atheist whose life was so messed up that it would take a sovereign God to straighten it out.

*PLAN OF SALVATION USING THE ROMAN ROAD

Romans 1:16 - The **gospel** of Christ is the **power** of God unto **salvation** to **everyone** that believes. **"For I am not ashamed of the gospel of Christ: for it is the power of God unto salvation to every one that believeth; to the Jew first, and also to the Greek."**

Romans 3:16 - **None** of us are righteous enough to go to heaven without salvation. **"Destruction and misery are in their ways."**

Romans 3:23 – **Every one** of us have sinned, therefore, we **all** need Christ as our Savior. **"For all have sinned, and come short of the glory of God."**

Romans 5:8 - God loves us even though we are sinners. **"But God commendeth his love toward us, in that, while we were yet sinners, Christ died for us."**

Romans 6:23 - "...the wages of sin is *death*; but the *gift of God* is eternal life through Jesus Christ our Lord."

Romans 8:1 - Everyone escapes the penalty of his or her sin through Jesus Christ. **"There is therefore now no condemnation to them which are in Christ Jesus, who walk not after the flesh, but after the Spirit."**

Romans 10:9 - Confess your faith in Jesus, **believe** in your heart that He is resurrected from the grave, and **you will be saved** from the penalty of your sin. **"That if thou shalt confess with thy mouth the Lord Jesus, and shalt believe in thine heart that God hath raised him from the dead, thou shalt be saved."**

Romans 10:13 - Anyone who **prays** for salvation **will be saved. "For whosoever shall call upon the name of the Lord shall be saved."**

Romans 12:1 - Live out your remaining days in **faithful** service to **Christ. "I beseech you therefore, brethren, by the mercies of God, that ye present your bodies a living sacrifice, holy, acceptable unto God, which is your reasonable service."**

5

A NEW CREATURE IN CHRIST JESUS

THE FOLLOWING SUNDAY Pastor Meek was shocked to see Don walk through the doors of the church. For the next few weeks, Don was down at that altar each time the invitation was given. The Lord seemed to deal in his heart about something new each service, but Satan began to work too. Remember, he was losing one of his prime workers. The following are Don's own words taken from a message that he preached in the 1980s:

When Brother Jeff Meek led me to Christ, the church was a new church, and they had only about twenty-five people. So after I got saved, Brother Meek would come by every Thursday night and visit me. I always had a list of questions that I wanted to ask him: Should you smoke? Should you drink? And things like that. I was so ignorant of the Word of God. I only knew two scriptures when I got saved. One was "God helps them that help themselves." And the other one was "A bird in the hand is worth two in the bush."

Now for those of you who are not laughing, those aren't really in the Bible and are not scripture verses. But all my life I was told that those were in the Bible. After I presented myself for baptism, Pastor Meek told everyone to go by and give me the right hand of fellowship. I had so little understanding of the things of God that I thought that by shaking their hands, I had just been baptized.

One Thursday night, after about three or four weeks, Brother Meek didn't come by to visit me. I had my list ready, and to make matters worse, someone at church had hurt my feelings. So the old devil started in on me. I thought, "Brother Meek loves those guys more than me, and he just really doesn't care about me." I really got offended. The old devil has a way to blow things up in our minds. He can make a mountain out of a molehill really fast. Now the devil had something ready for me that I really wasn't ready to handle. We expect Satan to attack us one way, but he always has about a dozen other ways to do it. I had a pet peeve before I got saved. Everyone has something that bugs you, something that really bothers you. Remember, I'm Jewish. What bothered me was for someone to go to the refrigerator, get out a package of cheese, cut a little bit off, leave it open, put it back in the refrigerator, and it would dry out. That would really set me off. It was Saturday morning. I'd gotten up, my feelings were already hurt, Preacher hadn't come to see me, and I was in a bad mood anyway. I went to the refrigerator, and there it was! That package of dried-up cheese. I opened the back door, and I tried to throw that cheese over our seven-foot redwood fence. It hit the fence, and I went charging out after it. I kicked that cheese all over the backyard until I had demolished it. But the shame of it was I was cussing while I was doing it. I said, "That's it, I quit. I'm not going crazy over some religion." I didn't get dressed all that day, and Sunday morning came, and I didn't get dressed again and didn't go to church. Brother Meek came by and told me that they had missed me at church. I looked at him and told him that was not the half of it. They would miss me from now on. I wasn't going back, and I meant it. He talked to me for quite a while and said he'd come by and pick me up for church that night. I told him that he could come by, but I wasn't going. He came right on time, but I was still in my robe. Somehow or other he talked me into it. I sat back in the corner and was puffed up like a toad, but God really dealt with me. I went down to that altar and asked God to forgive me for being angry and mostly for cussing and using His name in vain, and by His grace I continue on until this day.

But Satan, the accuser of the brethren, really works over a new Christian. "It couldn't be true that you are forgiven. How could you have forgiveness of all those sins? You're not fit to go to Heaven. There's no way a reprobate like you can go to there." New Christians have a problem like that with forgiveness of sins. I had a problem with it. I lived twenty-six years for the devil, and when I lived for him, I never spared the horses. I used to have a nickname before I was saved: "Put me down, I'll go Espinosa." If they wanted to have a wild party or a poker game, they knew that the first name on the list was Espinosa. They'd call and say, "Hey, let's have a poker game tonight." I'd tell them, "Put me down, I'll go." They'd say, "Let's go to Vegas." I'd say, "Put me down, I'll go." If they said, "Let's go to Tijuana," I'd say, "Put me down, I'll go."

I was always ready to serve the devil, and I had given him the best that I had. I can't understand why people, when they get saved, are unwilling to give the Lord what they gave the devil. All he ever gives is heartaches and miseries. The Lord wants to bless you and use you. I lived a wicked life. When I got saved I read the book of Isaiah, verse eighteen of chapter one. It is one of the first verses that I learned. It's talking about forgiveness of sins once a person comes to the Lord Jesus Christ: "...**though your sins be as scarlet, they shall be white as snow...**" When I read this, I thought about the time when I was eighteen years old and a soldier in France. We would have to go three and four weeks between getting clean sheets. And my sheets would get pretty bad by that time. When they put on the bulletin board that we could come get clean sheets, I'd run over there and go back and make up my bed. That night I'd take a shower before going to bed. I'd wash off my *feet again before I'd get in bed, I'd get up on the bed and slide my feet up and down the blankets to get off any dust or dirt that might have gotten on them, and then I'd slide down into those clean sheets. I didn't want anything to dirty them up. When I got saved and realized that my life had been cleansed and I was as white as snow, I didn't want anything to dirty up my life like that again.*

After his salvation Don was amazed at the peace and joy he had. He wanted everyone to be this happy and couldn't believe they wouldn't want what he had found. He wanted to tell everyone about this new joy. Don said, "I was like a human tape recorder. The preacher would preach a message on Sunday, and I would literally go and preach the same message to my friends. I'd see billboards and think of an illustration that I could use. Messages were always going through my mind. I thought this was normal for all new Christians. I began to ask other Christians if they wanted to preach. Their answer was usually an emphatic 'NO!' I never really surrendered to preach; I just began preaching."

For a while he continued to bowl. He had obligations to fulfill, but now everything was different. His bowling friends began to call him "Apostle Don," because he was always talking to them about the Lord. Don said they would laugh and say, "You ought to be a preacher." "I'd say, no way! I couldn't be in front of a group of people and do that." But that was exactly what God was preparing Don to do. Brother Meek gave him the opportunity to preach at his church. Don invited all of his old bowling friends to come, and of course they promised they would come to hear him. Don said, "That was the worst message anyone had ever preached. Remember that I quit school because of having to give oral book reports. So, needless to say, I was very nervous to be in front of a crowd, but I wanted my friends to hear the Gospel. I prepared my whole message on salvation. Do you know how many showed up? None! I looked at Pastor Meek and asked him what I should do. All of the people in the congregation were saved people, and my message was just for lost people. He just told me to preach what I had. I stumbled and stammered around, and nothing made any sense, not even to me. But the second time he told me I could preach, it was like I opened my mouth, and God spoke through me. I can remember thinking, 'Man, this is fun.' After that when I would get nervous, I'd look up at the moon and the stars and pray, 'If you're big enough to make all of that, you are certainly big enough to help this preacher.'

Where before he'd been the life of the party—the old "Put me down, I'll go Espinosa"—was different now. He'd go up to the bar to celebrate with his team after they won a match, but while they drank their beers, he'd sit and drink a cup of coffee. Don became more and more uncomfortable in this kind of atmosphere. He really began to understand the change in himself. It hurt him to hear the Lord's name in vain. Before his salvation, every other word out of his mouth was the Lord's name in vain. He asked his friends to stop doing it. As you can imagine, those friends began to scatter.

The old Don never had enough money, because he'd drink and gamble it all away. He was always borrowing money from his friends. There were men at Douglas Aircraft he'd owed money to for years. Now, all of a sudden, he had more money than he knew what to do with. He wasn't spending it on drinking, smoking, gambling, or going to Vegas. He became under conviction about the money he owed, so he went back to those at Douglas and paid off his debts. They could hardly believe the change in him.

Don just wanted to serve the Lord and do what was right. Since he worked nights, he would go on visitation with the preacher during the day. He helped enclose a garage to make Sunday school classrooms, and in the next apple orchard contest, he brought forty-eight first-time visitors to Sunday school. People were getting saved, but he had never won anyone personally. He began to have a battle within himself, and a good friend of his, Lester Young, showed him some scriptures on the old nature and the new nature. He finally understood this struggle within himself. He wanted so badly to win someone to Christ. He thought about that Christian parking attendant who used to leave the Christian station turned on so Don would hear it as soon as he started his car. He began to do this so his current parking attendant would have to listen for a little bit each day. He began to witness to this man and finally won him to Christ. He was so thrilled. He understood the joy one receives winning a soul to Christ. He was hooked.

At the time of Don's salvation, he was married to a woman much older than he was. They had supposedly married in Mexico after a drunken party. She wanted a hip, younger man, and he fit the bill to a T. She made a profession of faith at the same time Don did, but it never reached her heart. Shortly after his salvation, he had to go to Vegas for a bowling tournament. He asked her to go along so they could get legally married this time. She went, but afterwards she became more and more belligerent with him, cussing and yelling at him. She began locking him out in the evenings when he would go out soul-winning with the preacher. Many times he would take some friends over to the preacher's house so they could hear how to get saved. She would be furious at him. It never had bothered her before when he was out all night gambling, but now she was embarrassed of him and didn't want him around her friends. He was brokenhearted. He wanted to serve the Lord.

One Sunday Don went forward during the invitation. The pastor asked why he was coming forward. He replied that he really wasn't sure, but God was dealing in his heart about something. Brother Stone then asked him if he thought that maybe God was calling him to preach. He decided right then that this was what he should be doing, but his wife said there no way was she going to be a preacher's wife. Don and Brother Stone began to pray that God would change her heart, but she only became colder and more indifferent to him. Just a couple of weeks after they began to pray this prayer, she was diagnosed with leukemia and passed away less than five months later. God was preparing Don's life little by little to be used in a mighty way, but first he must suffer loss and persecution.

6

IF IT'S WORTH DOING, DO IT NOW

HAVE ANY OF you ever decided your life's journey in fifteen minutes or less? Well, that about sums up what Don and I did on May 2, 1964, but let's back up a little.

In September 1963, I met a handsome, dark, young man with the nicest smile I'd ever seen. He just seemed to be happy all over.

At the time I was surprised, because I had recently heard that he'd lost his wife to leukemia, but here was a man who really had the joy of his salvation. He'd been saved for only a year and a half, and during that time he had lost every possession he had except for his little six-year-old daughter, Donna. For the time being, she was living with a loving family from his home church.

When Don first came to Baptist Bible College, he joined up with a group of young students called the "Centurion Light." They had a burden for soldiers, and every Saturday they would go to Fort Leonard Wood army base to witness and win souls. They had a rally each Saturday night at the local Baptist church. The pastor was my father, and before the service my mother would prepare wonderful meals for this group of young men. One Saturday she asked Don to take a letter to me in Springfield. I'm not sure why she picked Don, but it was how I first met him.

About this same time, there were several of us college girls who needed rides to work. We worked as maids, all in different homes but in the same general location. One of the girls who needed a ride was from Don's home church. We asked her to approach him about driving us to our jobs. Many of the young men did this to earn a little extra money. He agreed, so eight of us piled into his Ford Falcon each day at 12:30 p.m. I was the last one on the route, and I was fifteen minutes farther out. I never could figure out his reasoning, but he would always pick me up first. This meant that there were fifteen minutes more before the other girls were picked up. This also meant that there were thirty minutes a day that Don and I were alone in the car together. Now that may sound wonderful, and your thinking is probably along the lines of "Oh, that's how they got together and fell in love." Not quite! You see, the summer before, I was working two jobs, sometimes fourteen hours a day, and going to summer school to make up some credits. During that time I wandered further and further away from the Lord. I even dated an unsaved young man. I was able to attend church only on Sunday mornings, because I was working during all of the other services. I was so tired all the time that I usually slept through those Sunday morning services. I had become very backslidden, angry, and indifferent. It took Don about five minutes the first day to pick up on my spiritual condition, and it became his mission, in those thirty minutes each day, to preach to me and try to get me back on track spiritually. There were days when I was so furious at him (actually, most of them) that by the end of January, I was so angry and miserable that I knew things were coming to a head. I dreaded the ride to work, because I knew what he was telling me was true. He never let up! The last day of the semester he gave it to me with both barrels.

He said, "Cherie, do you know what is going to happen to you if you don't get your heart right with God?" (He actually thought that I wasn't even saved.) "You are going to graduate in a few months, get out in the world, and marry someone who is unsaved and ruin your life." I knew he was right, and I really didn't want that kind of life. That weekend I heard three messages on backsliding—one from a college student, one from a missionary, and the last from my pastor, Brother Tom McGath. By the time he finished the message on Sunday night, I knew I would die right there in the pew of a heart attack if I didn't go forward and get my heart right with God. I left that altar, went home to my dorm room, and prayed nearly all night. I literally emptied out my heart and gave my life entirely over to the Lord. I couldn't wait to see Don the next morning to tell him and to thank him for not giving up on me. He looked at me and said that I was literally glowing. He rejoiced over my decision nearly as much as I did. He asked me to go soul-winning with him the following Friday night. Well, what can I say? It was love. We started and ended each date with prayer. That became the pattern for our lives together. We not only prayed together, but we'd read our Bibles and go soul-winning together, and then, we'd go to A&W for hamburgers, McDonald's for french fries and coke, and finally to Consumer's Market for chocolate éclairs. We were poor but happy.

We had our first date on February 2, 1964. On the second of May, Don was going to be preaching in a little church in Cuba, Missouri. I decided to go to my parents' home that weekend, where Don was staying. I'm afraid I was a little bold in doing that, but I wanted so badly for Don to ask me to marry him. I didn't want to miss out on a chance to be with him, so Sunday morning we went together to the little church in Cuba. The pastor introduced us as Mr. and Mrs. Espinosa. I blushed, and Don got up and said that we weren't married, but it sounded pretty good. That night, on the way back to Springfield, he pulled over on the famous Route 66 and asked me to marry him. In the next fifteen minutes, we decided that instead of waiting all summer to get married, we would do it on May 22, the night after I graduated from Baptist Bible College. We turned around and went back to tell my folks. They cried, Don cried, and I laughed. I was so happy I could hardly believe it.

Don always laughed about us getting our marriage license. Back then it cost only $3.50, and they gave us a bag of silver polish, dish soap, and other household goods. He'd say, "I only paid $3.50 for her, and they threw in a bag of groceries too. I think I got a pretty good deal."

I graduated on Thursday night, we were married on Friday night, participated in my sister's wedding on Saturday, left for California on Sunday, arrived on Tuesday, found an apartment that evening, picked up Donna—Don six-year-old daughter—and started our lives together. Don's motto was, if it's worth doing, do it now! So we did it and never regretted that decision for a second.

Don's pastor, Don Stone, made much of this possible by loaning us his gas credit card for the trip and giving us a $65 love offering from Don's home church, Bethel Baptist of Garden Grove. He also paid the first month's rent on our furnished apartment. We had $2 left when we arrived in California, and Don didn't have a job yet. Funny thing was I didn't even think about the financial part of it, because I knew that somehow Don would take care of me. I'd always been very poor, so not having much never bothered me.

One of the men from the church sold Fuller Brush products door to door. He asked Don if he would like to be on his crew of workers. Don figured if this man could support a family of ten selling Fuller Brush products, surely he could support the three of us. And he did and did it very well. We discovered a new gift that Don had: selling! He practiced his demonstrations on Donna and me, and we'd give him a hard time in return. It was a fun time and a great summer. Donna and I would deliver the products to his customers on Fridays and Saturdays so he could continue to work those two days. He had a wonderful neighborhood in Long Beach, and we loved helping him. We'd meet up with him at lunchtime and have a picnic in a nearby park. He was so pleasant and not pushy, and his customers really looked forward to him dropping by each month. Even though his customers did not know at first that I was his wife, I never heard one complaint about him. It was so amazing watching the Lord supply our needs that summer, and we had such a wonderful time.

When we left California to go back to Springfield, Missouri, we were no longer two. Now we were three with a baby the way. Don had never planned to remarry when he first went to Springfield. He'd had plans to be an evangelist, but now his life and desires had drastically changed. He was married with a family and had changed his major to missions. There had never been two people brought together who were so opposite in personalities, in spiritual backgrounds, in family, in the way we were brought up, and especially in the ways of the world. He'd always lived in the world until his salvation, and I had never experienced much of the world at all. One would think we would have had some real issues between us. Surprisingly, we didn't. The one thing we did have in common was that we had both grown up with fighting in our families. We didn't want that kind of marriage. We were so grateful that the Lord had brought us together that other things just weren't important. After we had been married for a while, I was thinking back over all God had to do to get us together. I knew that Don had been saved on a Friday night, October 13, 1961. At that time I was engaged to a young man from my home church. He was in Korea in the army. When I went to Bible College, I knew in my heart he was not the man God wanted me to marry. I fought a battle with the Lord for the first nine weeks of school. On the last Friday night of the semester, I couldn't fight it any longer. I wrote to him and told him I knew that he wasn't God's will for my life. When I was thinking back about the date Don got saved, I got out an old calendar and looked up what the date had been on that last Friday night of the first semester. It was Friday, the thirteenth of October. I could hardly believe it. While I was writing that letter in Springfield, Missouri, Don was being dealt with by Brother Jeff Meek in Westminster, California. God was already preparing the man that He would have me marry three years later. Some people might say, "What were the odds of that happening?" I'd say it was all in God's plan and in His time. With God nothing is impossible.

That first summer I met some of Don's old bowling friends. He was still trying to win them to Christ. I was told numerous times that if I'd known the "old Don," we probably never would have married. I knew that was probably true, but then again I didn't know the "old Don." They'd tell me that he had really reformed, but his life had been not reformed, but transformed!

7

LEARNING TO TRUST GOD

JUST TWO WEEKS before leaving California to return to Springfield, Missouri, Don bought an old station wagon from a friend. It had an electric rear window. We packed everything we owned in that station wagon. We'd roll up the window a little bit and stuff more things in and then roll it up some more until we had that car so full that you could not get one more thing in it. About an hour into our journey, the motor blew up. In one of Don's messages on trials he said:

> Before I was saved, I would have just blown up and kicked everything in sight, but knowing that **Romans 8:28—"And we know that all things work together for good to them that love God, to them who are the called according to his purpose"**—is true, I knew that this would somehow work out for our good. How could it be for our bad? You either trust God's Word, or you don't. I've found out that trusting God's Word is the only way to go.

We got back to our friend who had sold us the car. He rebuilt the motor, and a few days later, we were on our way again. This time we made the journey without incident. We never found out what God's purpose was for the breakdown, but it was sure a blessing that it broke down close to where we could get help and not out in the middle of the California desert.

Because of the delay in arriving back in Springfield, we had only a few days to find a furnished apartment or something to rent. We looked and looked and couldn't find anything. A couple of days before classes began, my sister and I went out to look at an unfurnished house. We were getting a little anxious, to say the least. By this time we didn't care if it had furniture or not. We'd take anything and do the best we could to gather up some furniture. A man who owned a dry cleaning business across the street had the keys to the house. Before he showed it to us, he said, "It's too bad that you aren't looking for a furnished place, because I have a completely furnished house that was just vacated." I couldn't believe what he had just said. We quickly told him it was exactly what we were looking for. He took us out to see the house, but he didn't have a key to get in. He crawled through an open window. The house was perfect, and I was absolutely amazed at what God had opened up for us. But Don was very leery of a landlord without a key. He had come from a long line of con men, and he thought for sure that this man was one of them. He figured this man had found a house that the owners had left for a short while or something to that affect. We went next door and talked to the neighbors. Sure enough, this man owned this house, and he had gotten divorced and was now living at the dry cleaners and renting out his house. We could spend only sixty-five dollars a month on rent. Guess how much he was asking? You got it—sixty-five dollars! We paid the rent, pulled the station wagon up to the back door, and moved in that afternoon. We were desperate for a place to live, BUT GOD! knew just what we needed and more. I had never lived in a house this nice in my life.

Don tried selling Fuller Brush products in Springfield, and it worked out great until the weather turned cold. No one wanted to stand and talk with their door open to a Fuller Brush salesman. We always had friends over, and Don got a crew together from his old college buddies. They all tried selling Fuller Brush, but they couldn't get anything going either. It was just too cold to be doing this, but those training classes in our front room were so much fun, and we'd have a great time doing them. However, things became very scarce. God was teaching me to trust Him. I saw the faith and trust that my husband had in the Lord to supply our needs, and he had been saved only a couple of years. I was learning how to completely trust God in every situation. Don was such an example to me.

During his first year, he had been interviewed by a Jewish man named Dr. Sanford. Dr. Sanford went to different Bible colleges and presented the ministry of missions to the Jews. He was looking for young Jewish Christian men to enlist them in possibly working for the American Mission Board to the Jews. They also helped out young Jewish pastor students with scholarship funds. It had been several months since Don had this interview, and we had actually forgotten about it. We were on our last twenty-five cents, and we had no idea where the money for our next meal was going to come from. The mailman came, and I went out to get the mail. There was a letter from the American Mission Board to the Jews. We were excited. Don said for me to open the letter and see what it had to say. It was a check! I thought at first glance it was for $25. We were thrilled to death for that. Then, when I gave the check to Don, he laughed and said to take another look. It was for $250. We couldn't believe it. We felt like millionaires. We went out and bought half a beef and rented a food locker. For the next few months, we just happened to have visitors from the college every night at suppertime. It didn't take long for the word to get out that the Espinosas had meat! The half a beef didn't last long, but we had such a great time with those students coming by each evening.

Another great thing came out of the interview with Dr. Sanford. He wanted Don to work for the summer for the American Mission Board to the Jews. They wanted him to work in one of their field offices in Hollywood, California. As soon as classes were finished, we packed up our young family and headed for California. They had made arrangements for us to live in a small apartment in LA on a Missionary Alliance Mission's compound. We didn't want to lose our wonderful house in Springfield, so we sublet it to five male students from Baptist Bible College. What a group this was. We wondered what we would find when we returned, but for now this was the solution to our problem of not losing the house.

We were excited about this new adventure. The apartment was very tiny, but we loved it and made do with our now eight-year-old and two-month-old daughters. Life was an adventure and a learning process, and we wanted to get the most out of this experience as we could. This mission board was very different from what we were accustomed to. They would befriend their contacts who, of course, were all Jewish. They would hold a get-together with them, and the customary thing was for this contact to invite their group of friends and acquaintances. Then the representatives would mingle with the people and get to know them and try to win their friendship before ever beginning to witness to them. They would usually have a guest speaker who would teach on something about the Jewish religion and its comparison to Christianity. Then they would invite the people to attend a service at the board head-quarters. Many would be curious enough to attend, and here they would start presenting the Gospel to them a little at a time.

Don was not accustomed to working like this. He wanted to begin witnessing as soon as he would meet someone. The board would give him contacts to visit, to invite them to the meetings, and he would start witnessing to them right away. People starting getting saved, and everyone was really surprised. They asked Don to teach a class on soul-winning, and he was thrilled to do it. As the summer went on, though, Don could see some things that he and the leaders could not agree upon; therefore we decided it was best just to leave instead of causing a conflict.

We headed back to Springfield for Don's last year of college. We were pleasantly surprised at the wonderful condition in which we found the house. One of the young men had taken it upon himself to be the "mom," and he kept everything in great shape. In later years he became a very faithful, supporting pastor and even now, although he has retired, his church still supports the mission endeavor in Argentina. They've never missed a month. There will be many souls in heaven because of this wonderful man's faithfulness for so many years.

Don's last year at BBC was a really good year for him. He'd stay every day for a few hours to study in the library. He'd finish his homework for each day plus work on projects that were due at a later time. This left his weekends free to sell cookware. He worked for Luster Craft cookware and did great at it. He'd leave on Friday after his classes were over, and he'd go to Arkansas, which was his territory. Just as everything Don did, he did it with all his might. He found out the best way to get leads, and then he'd go after them. He would go to the local high school library and look up the graduates from the last year in the yearbooks. Then he would find out their addresses from the phone directories. Those were the girls who would now have jobs and would usually still be living with their parents and looking forward to getting married someday. Naturally they would have the funds to buy things for their hope chests, because they didn't have any bills yet. Don would never pitch his cookware to a girl by herself. She either had to have friends or her parents present. God blessed his diligence, his honesty, and his morality. He had lived in the world for many years, and he knew the dangers out there, and he always tried to avoid even the appearance of evil. I remember one time when we were still dating that Don was very upset at one of the Baptist Bible College students who was working at the local A&W drive-in close to the school. We had stopped in for a root beer after church visitation. The young man thought it would be a good joke to make the drink in the mug look like real beer. Don sent it back and told the kid never to do something like that again. Most people would have taken it as a joke, but he was so determined in keeping his testimony clean that he didn't want even the appearance of evil to be present. Sometimes even I didn't understand the importance of this stand until I began to learn about the kind of life from which he had been saved.

That last year went by quickly, and soon it was time for Don to graduate. His desire was to work with a pastor somewhere and really learn how to do the work of the Lord. He really didn't want to pastor right away, because he had seen the heartaches his home pastor had gone through. He wanted to be more knowledgeable about the ministry—not only how to do it, but how to evade problems—before he became a pastor himself. During Fellowship and Graduation week, they would have what they called "Chatters Corner." It was a time when the pastors who needed workers in their churches could come and interview the graduating students.

No one came to Don. He said in one of his messages that he really wasn't very marketable. He didn't have any experience working with young people, and he couldn't sing or lead music. I couldn't even play the piano, and together we just didn't have a lot to offer. He was really disappointed about it. Secretly, he felt like a lot of it was that he was pretty dark-skinned and really looked like his Mexican heritage. In the sixties that wasn't something that was real common in the ministry. I didn't realize that he felt that way until many years later. It had never been a matter of discussion in our home. He knew that God had made him exactly like he wanted him and God would use him in whatever way He choose to use him and in whatever place. We were willing to go anywhere and do anything in the Lord's work.

The following week Don heard a message on faith at our home church. Pastor Tom McGath was preaching, and he said that we all needed to step out and trust God to lead us and not sit around waiting for something to be dumped in our laps. He was talking to everyone, but it especially spoke to Don. He came home and said, "Honey, we are going to take off on Tuesday and head west." I won't lie and say that I was really happy and excited about it, but I told him that we'd be ready.

On Tuesday we had everything loaded into a small trailer, but I was pregnant and very sick that morning. We only had $135 to our name, and we had two children and one more on the way. I really believe that my nerves added to my morning sickness, and it had a big part in my feeling so bad that morning. We had stayed with some friends overnight, and they graciously said we could stay another day with them. Don went out that afternoon and sold two sets of cookware, and that gave us another $130 to help with our traveling expenses. On Wednesday, we left for parts unknown. We would hear about a church that perhaps needed an associate, and Don would call and the position would already be filled. We kept going west, and when we arrived in Long Beach, California, we knew that it was the place God had called us to serve Him. We knew there could be some potential problems because of his mother's dislike of me, but we also knew that God had a purpose in our being there.

8

GOD'S TRAINING GROUND

The last building we bought.

DON, OUR TWO daughters, Donna and Judy, and I arrived at the end of May and found an apartment in Stanton. We immediately started looking for a place to start a church. Don sold cookware for a while to make some money to live on, but he found out he could not legally sell it there without being hired by the local franchise.

Don was hired back at Long Beach City Hall as a draftsman. He'd worked there for a short time before going to Bible College.

The Luster Craft franchise there in the LA area really wanted Don to work for them. They offered to pay him a lot more than he had made in Springfield, but they also wanted him to travel. He told them no; he was not there to make a lot of money but to start a church, and he could not be traveling. He also felt that they were asking too much for their cookware, and he knew it would be dishonest for him to sell it at the price they were asking. They wooed him in every way possible, but he refused their offers.

At Baptist Bible College, he was taught to beware of two things: money and women. He was afraid of money and what influence it could have on him. He wanted to serve the Lord with all of his heart and didn't want anything to distract him from that calling.

Before he was hired back at Long Beach City Hall, things became very tight financially. There were times when we didn't know where our next meal was coming from, but God always supplied. One evening Don came in and said that he had only fourteen dollars until his next paycheck, and thirteen of those belonged to the Lord for our tithes. He took an offering envelope and put the thirteen dollars in it. That left one dollar to last for a week. He hadn't any more than closed that envelope when someone knocked on our door. It was a pastor friend, Burl Nelson, from Rialto, California, with boxes of food for us. Their small church had taken a "pounding" for us, and this was the result of it. There were many canned goods with money taped to the top of them, and we could hardly believe our eyes. God always came through for us. Those were blessed, precious times in our lives and in our marriage. God was teaching me to trust Him more and more. Don never doubted that God would supply our needs, but it was a little harder for me to learn this lesson. But praise God, He didn't stop working on me.

Don used to laugh and say that someday he would write a book called *How Not to Start a Church*. As we continue, you will be able to see the reason for that title. We had no money, no congregation to receive an offering from, and our home church could not help us much financially. They did what they could to be a blessing to us. We started looking for an adequate place to hold services.

There were twelve mortuaries in Long Beach, and all were active except one. The directors said we could use the chapel for services on Sundays. During the week we used the garage behind the mortuary to store the pulpit, songbooks, a couple of baby cribs, flannel boards, and a few other things. This seemed like a perfect solution, and it was free! The local newspaper gave Don a quarter-page write-up. It told of a local boy starting a new church just three blocks from where he was born. A good friend of Don's, Jim Petri, said he would come to the service on Sunday morning to lead the singing, and his wife would play the organ. They attended the early-morning service at their home church and then came to the funeral home to help us out. Don had invited all of his old buddies to the first services and of course, received lots of promises.

We printed up flyers and passed them out. We put them in the local stores in the area. We'd gone door-to-door inviting people to come and were excited, but nervous, as we waited that first Sunday morning to see the results of our efforts. As the service began, we actually had fifteen people there. We'd hoped for more but were happy to have fifteen. One was a sweet, older lady named Clarisse Harris. This precious Christian lady attended faithfully for many months. She had been saved in a Billy Graham revival when she was just nineteen years old, and she was one of the godliest women I have ever known. She became someone I wanted to pattern my life after. I hoped someday I would know the Word of God as she did. She was such a tremendous blessing to us.

Another one of the fifteen was a beautiful, young Christian girl. In one of Don's messages, he was telling about this first service.

When I saw this beautiful young woman come in, I thought, "Oh, no, Satan has sent in that Jezebel we were warned about in Bible College to try and trip up my life and my ministry." In Bible College they told us that there were two things that could easily ruin our ministry, and they were money and women. I was just sure that Satan had sent her in to do just that so I didn't look directly at her all the time I preached. I was trying to preserve my family and my ministry.

This young woman actually turned out to be another blessing to us. She became my Sunday school helper until she had to return to college in the fall. That first service was really an eye-opener for us. We had expected more people to come, but God was already beginning to teach us lessons on trusting Him to keep His Word.

The first Sunday night we were in for a shock. Just as the service started, a man came into the vestibule and stood at the back of the chapel. Being a funeral home, the chapel was not brightly lit, and Don couldn't see who the man was or what he was doing. All of a sudden, this man came running down the aisle yelling, "Help me, help me!" He fell at Don's feet and grabbed hold of Don's pants and knelt there crying, "Help me, please help me."

Don was very shook up at this point, and I was scared to death. We could see that the man was on drugs and evidently hard up for another fix. Don pried the man's arms loose from around his legs, helped him to stand, and sat him on the front pew. He asked the man if he thought he could sit still for a little while until the message was finished. He would then take the man and get him something to eat. The man pitifully said that he would try and sit still. He sat there and shook and cried the whole time, but Don finished his message. He sent us home and took the man to get him a meal and then witnessed to him. The man made a profession of faith in Christ, but of course we won't know until the Lord comes back if the man really got saved or not, but he listened to the Gospel and prayed. We never saw him again. Thus began our ministry in Long Beach.

For three months we seemed to have fifteen at each service, but never the same fifteen. We'd laugh and say if we could get them all to come back at the same time, we would have a large crowd. We met in this funeral home for about seven months, but someone forgot to warn us that one month out of the year this funeral home was used by the county to hold services for people who couldn't afford to pay for them. Each of the twelve funeral homes in Long Beach dedicated one month of the year to this cause. One Sunday morning we were running a little late in getting to the funeral home, so Don hurried through the embalming room to the garage to get our nursery furniture. All of a sudden he stopped dead in his tracks, turned around, shut the door, and held his hand up. He looked at me and said, "Espy, don't go in there!" Being of Mexican descent, my husband was pretty dark during the summer months. However, this Sunday morning he was as white as a sheet. There was a body lying on the embalming table without any covering at all. Don had never seen a dead body before, and certainly not one looking straight up at the ceiling uncovered. Needless to say, he never again went running into that room without first checking to see what might be in there.

This incident took place just a couple of weeks before I gave birth to our third daughter, Shelley. When she was just six weeks old, something happened that shook Don's faith for a while. He had witnessed to his little Jewish mother ever since he had received Christ as his Savior, but she wanted nothing to do with the Lord. She only cared about gambling and having enough money to gamble with until she turned sixty-five. She could then start collecting Social Security. She had sold off all of the properties that she had inherited and was nearly penniless. The week before her death, she had gone to withdraw her last $500 from her savings account.

She would soon turn sixty-five and thought everything would be all right after that. There had been a mistake in her bank account book, and she actually had already withdrawn and spent that last $500. We told her that as long as we had food, she would have food. Don went shopping and took her a large bag of groceries. The next afternoon, he realized she had left that bag of groceries in our car. She only wanted money so she could satisfy her need to gamble. She was so addicted to it that she couldn't live without it. We were not about to give her money to gamble, but we would have definitely taken care of her physical needs until she received her Social Security. She was so distraught that she was broke, she had a heart attack. We went to visit her in the hospital, but she didn't want to even talk to us.

Sunday after church, Brother Jeff Meek came with his wife, Maudy, to try once again to win her to Christ. She seemed to be doing better that afternoon. On Monday morning I received a call from the hospital saying that Don's mother had passed away. The hardest thing I ever did was to call Don to tell him this. She had rejected Christ once again on Sunday when the Meeks visited her. Don was so shaken that his little Jewish mother had died without Christ that he began to doubt the power of God to answer his prayers. He had never stopped praying for her salvation, and now, as far as we knew, she had died and gone to hell. It took him a while to get over the shock of all of this. He just couldn't understand the reason that God did not answer the most important prayer of all, and that was for his mother's salvation. But it really gave him an understanding of the choice that people have to make for themselves. He understood how important his job was to preach and present the Gospel to everyone, but ultimately they had to make the choice of receiving or rejecting Christ.

Years later Don preached one of the most powerful messages that I ever heard on his call to Argentina. He preached using the text in **II Corinthians 5:14-15: "For the love of Christ constraineth us; because we thus judge, that if one died for all, then were all dead: And that he died for all, that they which live should not henceforth live unto themselves, but unto him which died for them, and rose again."** The love of Christ constrained us to go, because "there was a call from within, a call from without, a call from above, and a call from below."

He used the story of the rich man who cried out from hell for someone to go to his brothers to warn them. Don would use his mother's cry from below to not let Dolores, his sister, die without Christ, and for the thousands of Argentine souls that needed to hear the Gospel so that they wouldn't die like she did without Christ. Just telling about that message brings back the tears of watching Don go through this agony, knowing the torments that his mother was enduring for all eternity. God mercifully restored Don's faith in His power, not only to answer his prayers, but to trust Him to take care of our every need.

After seven months of using the funeral home, we decided to look for something else. We found an old Masonic Temple that had some rooms they could loan us. By this time we had several older ladies who regularly attended the services. The problem was the auditorium was on the third floor. We had to use an old elevator to get up there. But it would always stop about two feet short of reaching the third floor. Those dear little grandmas couldn't climb out of the elevator half the time. Every Sunday morning we would also have to clean up beer cans that had been left there by people who had used the facilities for parties the night before. Consequently we stayed there for only three months.

By this time we had enough offerings coming in that we could rent a building. We found a beautiful facility that was actually a dance studio. It was large, bright, and had rooms we could use for Sunday school. We were thrilled after being in those dimly lit places for the last year. While Don was preaching that first Sunday morning, he saw that people were not really looking at him but beyond him.

As a dance studio, the room was surrounded by mirrors that proved to be a great distraction from the message; therefore we bought large white sheets that week and covered all the mirrors around the room. That room was always decorated for the different seasons, and we never knew what we would find hanging from the ceiling each Sunday: a Christmas tree in December, a top hat and large champagne glass in January, a four-leaf clover in March, witches and black cats in October.

We began to grow and see a number of souls saved. There were a few who were always looking for someplace new to add to their lists of churches in which they could find fault. We had people from Tennessee, Kentucky, Missouri, Arkansas, Oklahoma, and a few other places. They were all looking for greener pastures. Don, a born-and-bred Californian, had a hard time understanding this new group of Bible-Belt Christians. They seemed to want to have the meat of the Word but acted like baby Christians, always getting their feelings hurt and needing to be pacified.

We had Dr. R. O. Woodworth come and preach a meeting for us. Don talked to him about these problems and how hard he was trying to help these parishioners and how much time it was taking. Brother Woodworth gave him the best advice Don could have ever received. He told Don to forget about running after these disgruntled people and just go out and win souls. Furthermore he told him to teach the new converts and train them, and then he would see the difference. That was just what Don did. He loved those people, but he had wasted so much time trying to heal up their hard feelings that he couldn't get anything else done.

We kept looking for a more permanent place to have services, and a storefront building on a main avenue became available. We had some new Christians and some now older Christians who were willing to do anything to help in the Lord's work. We rented the storefront, and for several evenings all the men and many of the ladies worked at this new location building walls for classrooms, laying carpet, painting, and whatever else was needed to get the building ready to use. It was such a joy, and the spirit was phenomenal. We worked so hard, but Don was still learning about many aspects of the ministry. He didn't get a rent contract, and we were in the building for only three months when they sold it right out from underneath us. Here we were again, looking for another place.

The Seventh-day Adventists let us rent their facilities for Sunday services since they were only being used on Saturday. We met in our home for the Wednesday-night prayer meeting, kept on with Thursday visitation, and continued looking for something permanent. Don once jokingly made the statement that if someone missed one Sunday they'd be lost forever, because they wouldn't be able to find out to where we had relocated.

After a few weeks, we found a church property for sale. It had an auditorium that would seat 105 people. They had the old wooden theater-type seats that were connected. It also had an apartment upstairs we could use for classes, and there was another building in the back of the property for the nursery and more classes and a large upstairs room for junior church. We were really excited this time. We bought this property, and Don attended Jack Hyles's pastors' school that March. He came back with both barrels loaded. Up until then we just couldn't seem to get more than fifty people coming at one time. Don said he felt like he'd been spinning his wheels for three years, and now he finally had a clue of how to build a great church.

We started a bus ministry, held Sunday school campaigns, had revival meetings, and did whatever it took to win souls. God gave Don a group of experienced pastor friends who really took him under their wings. They gave him such great counsel when he sought it, which he did frequently. He invited some great men in for revival meetings. We had Joe Boyd, Jim Lyons, Dr. Kenneth Gillming, Jack Garner, and others. Souls were being saved each and every week. It was wonderful. Don also had men come in to hold Sunday school clinics. One of these men was Don Ledbetter. He got our people excited about teaching and building up their classes and gave some wonderful ideas to carry out.

Don's right-hand man and first deacon was named Joe Hensley. Don had won this tough ironworker to Christ after visiting him week after week for three months. His wife had been saved in Dr. G.B. Vick's church in Detroit, Michigan. They moved to Long Beach, and Janice's mother had sent her a write-up out of the *Baptist Bible Tribune* about this young, growing church in Long Beach. Janice visited the church, and during that week we went to visit her at her home. We invited her husband to come, and to our surprise he did just that. Old Joe was a poker player, and each Friday night he'd have a poker game at his home. Don soon learned not to visit him on poker nights. But any other time was great. He really took a liking to Don and would listen to him. One night he bowed his head and prayed the sinner's prayer. From that time on he became Don's visitation partner. Together they won many souls to Christ. Joe's up in heaven with his pastor now, rejoicing with those souls they won to Christ.

For three years Joe and Don visited a man named Pete Block. Pete had insomnia and told Don to come anytime at all to visit him. Every Thursday night after they had finished their other visits, Don and Joe would visit Pete. He was really into racing boats, not just racing them but building them too. He and his wife, Patty, loved waterskiing, so every weekend that's where they were. But one Sunday Joe came dashing upstairs to Don's office before the service and said, "Guess who's here? Pete!" They had actually been dealing with two different men named Pete, so Don thought he was talking about Pete Holmes and not Pete Block. When he came into the auditorium, Don could hardly believe his eyes. There stood Pete and Patty. It had taken three long years of visiting them before they finally came. They didn't get saved that day, but on Tuesday evening Don and Joe went to visit them again, and they both gloriously received Christ as their Savior. Pete and Pat are still serving Christ to this day, and they have been instrumental in starting four churches. God greatly used these precious souls for His honor and glory. There were many others like Joe and Janice and Pete and Patty who were such a blessing to us and to the Lord's work there in Long Beach. We began to grow, and we hit a high attendance of 289 in those facilities. We had to have two junior churches going at the same time so there would be room in the auditorium for the adults and young people.

It was our first year in our own church facility that God brought the Faith Promise concept into our lives. We had supported missionaries from the beginning of our work, because our hearts were always in missions, but this actually began a new love for missions that involved the whole church. Faith Promise giving is asking God to show you what He would have you give and then trusting Him to supply that amount. Brother Jack Baskin came to preach at that first mission conference. We were amazed at the response from the church and excited to see how God was going to work among the people. During this time we also had the privilege of having Dr. and Mrs. Fred Donnelson come for a Sunday night. Brother Donnelson had been our mission teacher and the beloved mission director of the Baptist Bible Fellowship. He had been a missionary in China and had been imprisoned by the Japanese during WWII. What an impact he made on our church and on our lives that day. It was one of the greatest privileges we could have been given.

Don did everything possible to promote missions and keep the missionaries and the mission's offerings before the people. We set goals to reach each week as a church as well as in each class. We didn't actually have a clue, though, to the total impact that it would have in our lives. As I said in the first part of this book, our hearts had always been in missions. Don and I both graduated from the mission's course at Baptist Bible College. As soon as we started our church, we started supporting our first missionary family. A year after we started, we began using the Faith Promise missions plan. Four years later we were supporting twenty-five families all over the world. We would be thrilled when a new missionary would come through and present his field. We wanted the children to hear and learn about missions. We kept displays in each classroom, and everyone had a missions' offering goal to meet. Faith Promise not only gave our church a greater burden for missions around the world, but also for those who lived all around us.

Our church was diversified; many different nationalities attended. We lived in a mixed neighborhood, and our own kids grew up not really even knowing that there were many out there who were very prejudiced against the playmates and friends with whom they were growing up. I feel like this was another way that God was preparing our kids to be raised on a mission field without the slightest prejudice against their beloved Argentine friends. Although they are now separated by thousands of miles, many remain their good friends in their adult lives. Technology has made this a very small world.

After meeting in this building for three years, we knew it was time to find something much larger if we were going to continue to grow. We had reached our limit in this facility. God opened up the door to buy a large church property owned by the Church of Christ. We tried to raise the down payment among our people but lacked $10,000. Don called Pastor Kenneth Gillming and asked him if Cherry Street Baptist Church in Springfield, Missouri, could possibly help us out. They very graciously gave us the whole

$10,000. There were no strings attached, and we could hardly believe what God was doing.

We began working on the new buildings—painting, cleaning, and preparing the classrooms—with the help of our church family. We sent out thousands of invitations by mail to the areas around the church inviting them to the first service, which was to be held on Easter Sunday. What a great time of fellowship we had with those who helped in getting the facilities ready. We knew that God was going to honor the sacrifices of these dear people by filling up this building with souls. We felt like there was no limit to what God could do.

One funny, but very stressful, incident happened on the first Easter Sunday in our new building. We had acquired sixty little wicker chairs that were pretty worn. I wanted to spruce them up to make our beginner classroom bright and happy-looking. I painted all sixty of those chairs with enamel paint in bright orange, green, and yellow. I spent hours and hours doing this. I made posters for the walls and couldn't wait for Easter Sunday for the children to see their new classroom. They loved it and were happily sitting around the tables coloring and doing their projects when the bell rang to say that the class time was ending. As the children began standing up to get in line to go to their parents and to the buses, I suddenly noticed that there were smudges of green, yellow, and orange paint on their new Easter finery. I wanted to die right there on the spot. The paint had not dried in between the wicker fibers that were woven together to form the seat of the chairs. I tried to clean them up as much as possible but had to quickly write out notes telling the parents to please send the cleaning bills to us, or if they had to replace the garments we would pay for them. The parents very graciously accepted their ruined Easter finery without too much backlash. Don used to call these mishaps "Murphy's Law: Whatever can happen, will happen, so don't get too upset over it." We always tried to have a plan B in place when there might be possible problems with whatever we were doing. (I'm convinced our own kids really believe we lived by Murphy's Law.) We'd sometimes get down to plan B, C, D, and so on. I actually called us the "Keystone Cops," because that seemed to be the way we did many things. We got through those times by laughing, and believe me there was a lot of laughing through the years. For those of you who are young and don't know who the Keystone Cops were, they were comical policemen during the silent movie era who would get into all kinds of messes.

Most of our trials during those days in Long Beach were financial, and God taught us that we could totally depend on Him to get us through those trials, one way or another. We didn't have much materially, but we had joy, peace, and lots of love in our home in Long Beach. Our kids had their illnesses of sore throats, bronchitis, ear infections, and the chicken pox, but nothing too earthshaking. We were really happy and thought that God would use us there for the rest of our lives. But then came that day when Don came in with his question of "Where do you think God would want us to go if He opened the door for us to go to the mission field?"

Before we moved into this facility, a young reporter from the *Long Beach Press-Telegram* came out to interview Don. It really shows Don's character and what he planned to do.

ARTICLE FROM *THE INDEPENDENT PRESS-TELEGRAM*
Long Beach, California, Saturday, May 27, 1972
By LES RODNEY

"The old-fashioned gospel is what people are looking for. There's no satisfaction in modernism."

So says the pastor of one of Long Beach's younger and faster-growing churches. He is Rev. Don J. Espinosa, a 37-year-old local product who graduated from Poly High and City College and who will be remembered by bowling buffs as some kind of whiz on the alleys.

Starting from scratch less than five years ago in a downtown funeral home by Espinosa, his wife and a couple of friends, the strongly fundamentalist Bible Baptist Church has outgrown several other temporary homes, and this Sunday moves into new quarters at Tenth Street and Termino Avenue which it bought and renovated.

Espinosa trained for the ministry at Baptist Bible College in Springfield, MO., headquarters for a loosely knit fundamentalist fellowship which boasts some of the largest churches and Sunday Schools.

NATIONAL FIGURES show that, in general, while others are holding their own or declining slightly, the churches with vigorous growth patterns are almost always those with clean-cut adherence to basic doctrine, a conservative outlook, an intolerance for deviation, and a reputation for strong Bible-centered preaching. In brief, that old-time religion.

That is exactly where the personable young Espinosa is at. "An old friend of mine from years back is an elder in a United Church of Christ," he said with a sorrowful shake of the head as he showed me around the new church. "I just don't know how a fellow could go to a church that doesn't believe in anything." In his view that means most of the churches around Long Beach, except for a few that he named which he feels fulfill the requirements that a Bible-believing Christian should look for in a church home.

"Basically," he said, "there are three things—do they believe and teach and preach the Bible? Are souls won to Christ constantly? Is there a strong missionary emphasis?"

Most Southern Baptist pastors, for one, it was suggested, would list the same requirements. How would Bible Baptist Church differ from them?

There are many good Southern Baptist churches, Espinosa hastened to reply, but: "They are a denomination and a process of corruption sets in when you are a centrally controlled denomination. Another thing, you notice that Dr. Griswell, their former president and a good Bible believer, had to fight against liberal modernism in their schools."

And what if the Bible Baptist Fellowship, as it grows, follows the path of others and becomes a centrally-directed national denomination, subject to the influences which Espinosa sees as inevitable in denominationalism?

He shrugged. "We are not tied to anyone. We support the Bible Baptist Fellowship only so long as it is not modernist. Nobody tells us what to do but the Lord."

Bible Baptist's membership, after slow steady gains, picked up a head of steam in the past two years, he relates, with membership growing to solid 289 adults—mostly in the young married bracket—and the Sunday School jumped from 40 to 200, making the new quarters imperative. The pastor says he lists 389 professions of faith in Christ won during 1971 alone through weeklong crusades his church conducts.

As to where his members come from: "From many different backgrounds. We have folks here who were raised in churches that don't preach the gospel. They were religious, but lost. Sunday school teachers pledge not to smoke, drink or attend moving pictures. There's a lot of filth and immorality, he says, and adds with a smile: "I prefer old shoot-em-up westerns." In his sermons, he has attacked what he considers pornographic movie ads in this and other newspapers.

Bible Baptist Church is definitely not a candidate for inclusion in the local area Council of Churches fellowship. Espinosa does not believe in ecumenical good fellowship with any old church and its ministries.

"I can't sit next to someone who denies the Virgin Birth, the blood atonement, and the bodily return of Jesus Christ to the ear, and have fellowship with him," he explains with a patient smile, adding that the Bible is "very clear on this."

There are some people, he readily agrees, who may try Bible Baptist who might not be able to adapt to what they find.

What they will find, he makes clear, is, in addition to a friendly welcome, "strong preaching and a separation from worldliness."

"If people are used to just going to church to play church, I guess we might be too strong for them."

The church, he reports, has attracted not only Long Beach residents, but attendees as far away as Gardena. And it has some Black families along with the basically Caucasian majority.

"All are welcome here," Espinosa says, in the tone of *it's no big thing.* "The Lord said, whosoever will, may come, and that's what we say."

The reporter on this weekday morning found a group of energetic and cheerful volunteer workers helping to whip things into shape, including a nursery and a large classroom for team teaching, and getting out of a mailing.

Almost as if to underscore the pastor's casual reference to the racial mix, two young Negro women came in to join their white fellow members in the cheerful hubbub of preparatory work.

The newly located church is opening up with an eight-day "revival meeting," with Sunday services at 11 a.m. and 7 p.m. and weeknights at 7:30 p.m. There will be special music, the pastor says, though there was no organ in the church at the moment since the Church of Christ who formerly occupied the premises does not permit instrumental music in church. However, Espinosa finds no warrant for it in scripture.

"They didn't even have a piano," said Rev. Espinosa, not saying anything more about it but clearly enough indicating that this seemed pretty far out.

When I left, I ventured the suggestion that Bible Baptist church's moving days were over, at least for some years ahead. Rev. Don Espinosa shook his head negatively.

"Uh, uh," he said with a little smile. "We expect that one day we'll be holding our services in Municipal Auditorium."

I'm not entirely sure that he wasn't serious.

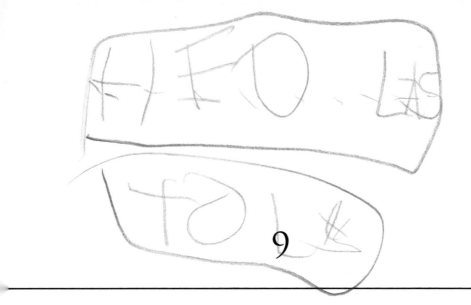

9

DO EVERYTHING DECENTLY AND IN ORDER

I SAID BEFORE when God opened the door for Don to do something, he literally ran through it and never looked back (although before going through that door, he always made sure it was God's will.) Before Don came to tell me that he knew that God wanted us on the mission field, he called several of his pastor friends who were older and had more experience in the Lord's work. He asked their advice about whether they thought he should go or not. After all, the church was growing, we had great facilities, and we were happy in the work in Long Beach. Don was actually past the age limit to be approved by the Baptist Bible Fellowship. (The Fellowship has since changed that age limit.) Some said they thought it would be great, while others said he should stay right where he was. He prayed and prayed about it. The decision came down to this: if he left the church in Long Beach, there would be plenty of good pastors who would be willing to step in, but if he didn't go to

Argentina, those people might never hear the Gospel. That was the deciding factor for him.

As soon as Don knew that God had opened that door to go to the mission field, he began the preparations. He called the Baptist Bible Fellowship mission office to ask for the application forms. We filled them out with much prayer. When we sent the forms back, the directors told us to come to Springfield for a candidate school.

At this time, Don went before our church in Long Beach and told them of our decision to go to Argentina. There were many tears that morning, because most of the people in our church had been saved there. This was our family, and we loved them very much. But they also loved missions and were happy that we were going to have this opportunity to serve the Lord on the foreign field. It was a scary time for us as well as for them. Don had been the only pastor that many of them had ever had. It was going to be a big change in all of our lives.

We were able to ride with a couple from California who was also going to the missionary training school. We had very little money to make this trip, so it was a big help. A friend said we could stay in his home while we were in Springfield. Although we really didn't have the means to do this, God, as always, provided. It was one very intense week of training and screening, but it was a great time…and a difficult time as well. We had to go through a battery of psychological screening, and for me that was a grueling time. There were things from my childhood that had had a very negative effect on me, and I was sure this would all come out in these tests. Don, on the other hand, just took it all in stride. He had one thing on his mind, and it was getting to the mission field as quickly as we could, because he knew it was God's will. The night after we took these tests, I could not sleep. I just knew that we would not be able to go, and it would be my fault. Satan really did a number on me that night, but Don just held me and said it was all in the Lord's hands.

As we each went in to see the results of the tests, sure enough, my fears were realized. There were no problems as far as our marriage was concerned, but in order for us to go to the field, I had to agree to go to group counseling to resolve the issues and negatives things in my heart and mind. I was willing to do anything we needed to do to get to Argentina. However, the big surprise came when they also said that Don needed group counseling too, because the tests showed that he was "hostile, angry, and depressed." We actually laughed when we heard the results of his tests. Don was the most upbeat guy in the world and had never suffered from depression in his life. But the hostile part did come out a little in the counseling sessions when he said he wanted to get everyone "straightened out doctrinally." The therapist indicated that pastors were making their congregations paranoid by pushing them to be soul winners. After some therapy sessions, this group felt that they were now free of these past convictions, because these convictions had been forced on them. Don asked the therapist about the people in the book of Acts who were saved on the day of Pentecost. They sold everything and went everywhere spreading the Gospel. He said, "I wonder how they would come out on your tests. This kind of reasoning really got to Don. He had lived a very wicked life of sin, and God had saved him and made him new creature in Christ Jesus. It was very hard for him to think of people wanting to be free from convictions concerning their Christian walk and how these convictions could have been forced on them. After three weeks the therapist said that Don didn't need to come anymore.

But that week in candidate school had some very positive things to offer. We learned how the mission office worked. We learned how to do deputation, how to write newsletters, how to get along with other missionaries, and many other matters. They also had some great Bible teaching on forgiveness and loving the brethren. Those lessons were lifetime lessons, and I praise God that we learned so many great things in those sessions. It was also a very emotional time as we dealt with spiritual issues in our lives. On the final day of the sessions, where many tears had been shed, Brother Jack Bridges, our mission director, asked some of us what we had learned or enjoyed and what we would really like to see change in our lives. After some tearful answers, he turned to missionary Lonnie Brooks and asked him what he had really enjoyed. Brother Brooks, with a completely serious face, said, "I really enjoyed the cinnamon rolls that they served." Brother Bridges stammered around, trying to get his composure while everyone was laughing, and he asked Brother Brooks what he would like to see done differently in his life. He said, "I would like my wife to learn to make those cinnamon rolls." That ended any serious discussion. And actually we *needed* to lighten up a little, because many there were emotional basket cases, myself included. It's funny how something like that would be the thing we remembered all through the years. I just recently spoke to Lonnie and Georgina Brooks, and he said that many people have reminded him of those two statements through the years.

We had to wait a couple of months until the September Fellowship meeting in Fairfax, Virginia, to go up for approval. Meanwhile, Don resigned as pastor of Bible Baptist Church, and we moved to Anaheim to live. One of our good pastor friends, Lyle Smith, had just taken a church in Bakersfield, and he let us rent his home in Anaheim for much less than it was worth. We were very fortunate that we did not have any debt. Remember, Don was raised by his Jewish mother, and she had taught him from a small child to never go in debt for anything. If you do not have the money for it, you don't need it. But here we were with no church salary and no support. We had to borrow $450 to buy tickets to fly to Fairfax.

But Don was so sure it was God's will that we would be approved that he began to line up some churches in the area to present our burden for souls in Argentina. By doing this, we had enough love offerings coming in to supply our most pressing needs.

In September 1972, we were taken before the subcommittee, then before the missions committee, and then presented to the fellowship for approval. Those were grueling days and very difficult for me, being a very shy, self-conscious person. Some of the issues that had to be discussed were my six weeks of group counseling, the issue of Don's age, taking an older teenage daughter to the field, and the language issue. Most just took it for granted that Don could speak Spanish because he was Mexican, but he couldn't. It was one of the hurdles that we would have to cross, and because of his age, it could be a problem. But after a long discussion with the missions committee, they decided to present us before the fellowship.

I'll never forget the kindness of Brother Lyn Chavez, who was an assistant mission director at the time. He came into the room where we were waiting, and he knew that I was very nervous and distraught after all the questions. He sat down on a chair in front of me and said, "I wanted to be the one to tell you that you are now Baptist Bible Fellowship missionaries." I'll never forget that moment. I felt as if God had just bestowed a precious gift on us to allow us to represent Him as missionaries in a foreign land. I was literally overwhelmed.

Don was happy, and he didn't waste any time. As soon as we were presented to the fellowship and the services were over, he was out talking to pastors and getting dates filled. By the grace of God, he was able to get many appointments that very night. Many of the pastors came to him and asked when he would be in a certain area. We had been advised to try and keep our deputation in one part of the United States—it would save a lot of time and money when returning for furlough and reporting to all of our supporting churches. For years Don always laughed and said that he kept his deputation in one area, the whole United States, but then he started receiving support from Mexico and from Costa Rica. It was no longer concentrated in one area! He actually had support coming from thirty-nine different states and two foreign countries.

10

GO FOR THE GOLD

"Go for the gold" was an expression that Don used all the time with our kids to encourage them to try to do their best in whatever they set out to accomplish. This was his attitude about getting his support. He wanted to get to the field as quickly as possible, but he did not want to go under- supported. He knew from pastoring that without funds a pastor cannot do much of a ministry. He has to have the means with which to do it. Don had a very organized mind. He made his plan and set out to complete it.

Don and I had heard of the horrors of deputation, but he always looked at things in a very positive way. His goal of getting to Argentina to reach the souls there was upmost in his mind. He set out to be a blessing to as many people as possible, pastors as well as the congregations. He knew there would be some trials involved, but he also believed that ahead of us were going to be multiple blessings. We had never been away from each other before this time. But for now, we felt that it was best for me to stay at home with the kids and for him to do the traveling alone. We had one daughter in high school, two daughters in grade school, and a three-year-old son. Homeschooling was a brand-new concept back then, and I had never even heard of anyone doing it. We felt that doing it this way was the best decision, especially for our oldest daughter.

This separation was the most difficult part of deputation as far as I was concerned. For the first time in over ten years of marriage, Don was gone most of the time, and apart from missing him terribly, I had to start taking care of bill paying, decision making, discipline problems, and dealing with a three-year-old who could not understand where his daddy was. Our little boy became very fearful and shy during this time. For the first few weeks, Don did deputation in California, so he was home most of the time at night. He was in a different church every service. If the church was close enough for us to go with him, we would go. Wanting to be good examples as missionaries, we insisted that the kids, including this little three-year-old, attended their corresponding Sunday school classes, and our son became more and more fearful. Praise the Lord that we finally realized what he was going through and started letting him sit with me during the services. There are different situations for each family, and each family has to make its own choices of what is the right thing for them to do.

One disadvantage we had was that we had absolutely no promised income to live on until Don was able to raise some support, but we did have the Lord! On our first report we had $50 come in, and that was actually from a businessman whom Don knew. The mission office gave us some advances and that really helped, but money became pretty slim sometimes. However, the Lord always came through. It's amazing how little a family can learn to live on. Even in Long Beach, we never really had much to live on, but our basic needs really didn't amount to much. Many of these lessons in trust had already been learned and proven, but sometimes our memories fail us. I've always been more of a worrywart, and I would get pretty shook up sometimes wondering how we were going to pay a certain bill or even buy groceries. We had been approved for two months by Thanksgiving. We had absolutely nothing in the house to eat let alone prepare for a Thanksgiving dinner. We thought if we could make do until Wednesday night, Don would probably get a good love offering, and we could buy some food for Thanksgiving. On Tuesday night Don and I were praying, and Don said, "Lord, you know our needs. We basically have nothing in the house to eat, and there are bills that need to be paid. Lord, we need a blessing. Oh, and Lord, don't send it through the mail. Do something really different this time." I sat up in the bed after he prayed and looked at him and said, "Are you crazy? We need it any way that we can get it." The mail was usually a pretty good source.

Well, Wednesday night came, and Don was preaching in a church that was a good distance from us. He came in really late that night. Meanwhile, there was a knock on the door, and a pastor friend from Anaheim was standing there. He and some men of the church had brought over several boxes of food they had taken up that night. Everything that you could possibly want to eat for Thanksgiving was in those boxes, plus several envelopes with cash in them. When Don came in, he took one look at all that food and turned and said to me, "It didn't come through the mail, did it?" That was one answered pray he never let me forget.

It was amazing watching the Lord supply our needs. Most of the time, it would come just on time, but it came.

Before starting out on deputation Don made up packets to send to each pastor who had shown an interest in having him come. These packets summarized what he had done in the past and what he hoped to do in the future. He would ask pastor friends to line him up in a certain area with their pastor friends. This actually worked out very well for him. He picked up a few churches in California, but after a few weeks, he decided it was time to branch out. He already had a few churches lined up on the East Coast, so he worked on lining up churches that would be more or less on a certain route across the states that he would be going through. One advantage was there were many of his fellow classmates from Baptist Bible College that had left college with the same burning desire that Don had to start new churches. Faith Promise giving was still a relatively new concept, and everyone was excited about it and the results they were seeing in their churches. Many of these new churches were actually looking for new missionaries to support.

As Don headed out driving across the United States, God began to bless. He picked up some support on the way, but it wasn't until he reached the East Coast that he really hit what he always called "his glory hole." This was a favorite expression he used when he was fishing. His pastor friends had come through for him, and out of fourteen churches where he preached in, he received support from thirteen of them. There were new churches being started all over the East Coast back then. It was a wonderful time to raise support, and God really was taking care of us. Don met many new preachers who became very close friends. There were also several pastors who had been in his class at Baptist Bible College.

Don had his share of unique experiences in his travels across the states. At night, if he didn't have a church close by where he was supposed to be, he would call up a pastor in the area and ask if they possibly had a missionary apartment where he could stay. Sometimes they did, and sometimes they would offer to put him up in a hotel. God always seemed to supply this need. He was put up in everything from a no-star to a five-star hotel. Sometimes when he would reach his destination, the pastor would tell him that he would be staying with a family in the church. This was fine, but many times he would have to leave in the morning and stay away all day until the husband came home that evening. He spent a lot of time in libraries!

Once he stayed in the home of two chiropractors, and that evening they both adjusted him. He laughed and said he felt like a pretzel when they were twisting him around. That night they put him in a very nice guest room. They forgot to open the heat register, which was under the bed. It was the middle of winter in Ohio. During the night he was freezing, and he looked around for an extra cover. He couldn't find anything, so he took the cover out of the dog's bed and used that. It's amazing what we will do when we are cold. The dog tried to pull it off of him during the night, and Don kept pushing the dog off.

A few days later, he was in another church, and the pastor and his wife had Don stay with them in their home. They gave Don their little girl's room. During the night the little girl came in and tried to get into her bed. Don felt the covers move, and he reached out. In his half asleep state, he felt the little girl's head, and he thought it was the dog from the chiropractors' house. He reached back to push the dog away, and the pastor came in and picked up the little girl and took her out. He thought about it later and said if he had backhanded that little girl, thinking she was the dog, he would have felt horrible, and there certainly would not have been any support raised there!

Another time he was sleeping in a room in the basement of the church. It had no windows, so it was pitch black when the lights were off. All of a sudden, he heard the telephone ring. He was very disoriented and thought he was in a hotel room. He jumped out of bed to answer the phone and ran right into the wall. He hit his head so hard he nearly passed out.

These stories went on and on, and he would tell them and just laugh. He always had such a good attitude, and in turn he taught all of our kids to make the best out of a bad situation. As they were growing up, it seemed like every time we had some kind of tragedy or hard thing happen to us, we would end up laughing about it. People would sometimes think we lacked a little something upstairs, but the humor brought us through some very difficult times.

That trip to the East Coast was seven weeks long, and we were both about to go "bonkers" being separated so long, as Don would say. He was in Maine at that time, and his next church was going to be in Detroit, Michigan, at Temple Baptist Church. He called and told me that he wanted me to fly up to Niagara Falls in Toronto, Canada, and he would meet me there so I could drive back across country with him. By the time I bought the ticket, the funds I had were completely depleted so I arrived with $2.00. We thought that he would have a love offering from the last church that he preached in to hold us over until we arrived in Detroit. We knew they always gave a $200 love offering, and that would get us back home to California.

Well, Murphy's Law was already in effect. The church in Maine only gave him an offering of $18.00, and it cost that much to buy gas to drive to Toronto. When I got off the plane, the first thing he said was, "I hope you brought some money, because I don't have a thing." I laughed and said, "I hope two dollars will do it." Well, of course it wouldn't, and we had a real dilemma on our hands. We had a credit card but did not have any line of credit to take out cash with it. We met up with my sister and her husband from Binghamton, New York. We ended up driving back to New York to go to their bank to try to see if they would give us some cash on the credit card. After several hours (no computers back then), we were able to get seventy-five dollars. After ten years of marriage, we finally had a wonderful honeymoon at Niagara Falls. We had a great time and a good laugh over our predicament there.

From September 1972 until June 1973 Don traveled alone. In June we traveled with him for four weeks in Colorado. It was a beautiful trip, and we were able to pick up some churches there. We took a survey trip to Argentina in July to get some idea of just what we were facing. We also wanted to get pictures that we had taken ourselves to put in the slide presentation. We were gone three weeks, and it was definitely a very profitable time. The pictures that we took as we traveled around the country made the presentation real, not only to us but to the churches. Don could actually show the souls that needed Christ as their Savior. One of the slides was of a dear old grandmother crawling on her hands and knees up a path in front of a Catholic church to light a candle to an idol of Mary that was located there. It gave us a greater desire to get there as quickly as we could.

When we returned from that trip, we moved to Texas to finish out our deputation. We lived there for four months, and Don was in a few mission conferences but mostly in a different church for each service. In fourteen months of deputation, he missed only one service, and that was on a Wednesday night. He used to say, "If I had to do it all over again, I'd move to Texas and do it all right there."

We had decided we would go to language school in Queretaro, Mexico. We bought a small seventeen-foot travel trailer and packed it with all of our household goods plus the kids' bicycles. We had attended Pastor Bill Slayton's church while in Texas, and they very graciously crated up our appliances and the few things that we were not taking to Mexico with us. On Christmas Eve we drove to Abilene, Texas, and spent Christmas with Don and LuJean Stone and their family. We left the following day to begin our next step of preparation, and that was language school. This turned out to be one of our greatest trials yet.

11

A PIECE OF CAKE: DON'S STRUGGLES IN LANGUAGE SCHOOL

THIS TITLE SOUNDS like a contradiction, and believe me, it is. Whenever the kids had a tough assignment in school and they just didn't think they could do it, Don would say, "It's a piece of cake." Well, the task ahead of him now— language school— didn't seem to be so hard. Mastering things always seemed to come easy to Don. And after all, he was Mexican, and speaking Spanish was in the blood. People actually said this to him many times. But then came the first day of language school. It didn't take him long to realize, that this was not going to be "a piece of cake."

After spending a couple of days with Bro. Don Stone and his family, we left Abilene, Texas, and drove several hundred miles south to the border. When we crossed the border into Mexico, we were all excited about this new adventure, but the anticipation of what was ahead was very scary to me. They gave us a booklet with words and phrases in Spanish we would need right away. For the next several hundred miles I studied these phrases and tried to pronounce them. I actually didn't have a clue what the sounds would be like. However, it was fun learning some of the new words and practicing them on the kids.

When we arrived in Querétaro, we met with the missionaries who were in charge of helping the new students settle into homes. The house they had for us had four bedrooms and four bathrooms. It had belonged to another missionary family. It looked very modern and was clean and ready for us to move into. We thought we had hit the jackpot with four bathrooms because of our three daughters and our son. But I don't believe more than two bathrooms ever worked at one time. There was usually just one in working order.

There were so many new things to get accustomed to. The missionaries tried to help us get settled. It was all very daunting and so different. They told us where the best place was to do our shopping, and gave us some tips on how to treat the beggars who inevitably would soon be at our door and at our car windows every time we left the house. All the windows on our house had metal bars on them. The entire house was surrounded by a tall fence with a huge iron gate. They warned us about letting kids take our shopping carts to the car to "help unload." They all looked so innocent, but were known to steal everything they could. Everywhere we turned there would be women sitting on the sidewalks with one or two babies in their arms begging, as we came out of the grocery stores. This was very hard to see. I remember one day when Don went fishing, and he brought the fish home to clean them. I wrapped the heads and entrails in newspaper, enclosed them in plastic bags and tied them tight before putting the bags outside the gates for the trash collectors. As I entered the house, I noticed some women walking by. In just a few seconds, they had taken those plastic bags with the fish heads and left. The next day, I asked our language teacher why they took the trash. She said that anytime you put fish heads in the trash they will take them home to make soup. It made me sick at my stomach to think about these pour woman having to use our garbage to make a meal for their families. After that I made sure that every fish head was washed clean. I put them in plastic bags first, and then wrapped the bags in newspaper. That way the garbage would at least be clean garbage.

I wanted to help everyone, but the missionaries warned us against this. They told us if we started giving food to the beggars, they would be back at our gate everyday—along with a dozen friends.

One huge blessing was the other missionary family, Leonard and Cindy Meyers, who would be studying with us. They were missionaries to Peru, and had children the same age as our three youngest ones. The kids became close friends very quickly, and we were grateful to have the Meyers there with us. We settled in and were ready to start language study.

There were only four couples in the school at that time: the two of us, who were starting first term, and two couples who were starting their second term. They told us the horror stories about the women crying when they had to get up and recite, and men who became angry and frustrated. I was a nervous wreck, but Don just seemed to take it all in stride. Then came the fateful first day, and Don knew that he was in for a hard time.

We went to school for five hours that morning, and then we studied for another four or five hours that evening. The next morning Don could not remember anything we had studied the night before. Needless to say, he was a little discouraged. Every day we would attend class, and every evening we would study together for several hours, but it just didn't seem to stick for him. He wanted to know why sentences were structured as they were, and what the reason was for this and that, and there didn't seem to be any answers. The teacher would just say, that was the way it was. His analytical mind just couldn't accept it. He wanted answers. He thought an explanation would help him to understand it better, but nothing seemed to help. The other couple was getting it all right, and I wasn't having too much trouble understanding and memorizing. This made it even harder on Don and his frustration level seemed to rise with each lesson. I began to see Don feeling worse and worse about the situation, and my husband, who had always been very positive in most situations, began to slip further and further into the proverbial, "slough of despond." I didn't know what to do or how to help him. All I could do was pray for him, and I tried to encourage him.

Every few weeks, we would have a short break from school. We took advantage of those breaks to get our family out of Querétaro, and see some of Mexico. It was a wonderful learning time for our family. We learned how the people made their living. Some women would weave blankets out of goat's hair, and they would use the goat's milk to make cheese. We would see the beautiful things they made out of wood. It seemed like each little village would specialize in making different things. We really began to look forward to those breaks. Many times we would go on a day trip with the Meyers.

One time we had a week off, and we went camping with the Meyers and another missionary family, the Stevensons, from Celaya, Mexico. We went to Lake Victoria, and it became Don's favorite place to escape. It had been a small town before the government had built a dam. They flooded the town that formed Lake Victoria, and stocked it with bass. Don and Leonard would sometimes take off for a couple of days just to go fishing there. They asked me to make them sling seats, which would attach around each side of an inner tube. They looked pretty silly, but those homemade slings did the job. One time Don was trying to get into his at the edge of the lake, but he became tangled up and turned upside down. His head was in the water, and his feet were sticking straight up in the air. We laughed until we were crying. Those two characters were hilarious together.

The first afternoon, I decided to walk down to the lake with our four-year-old son to see how they were doing. Don had found some styrofoam life preservers for the kids. He tied ropes around the life preservers and pulled the kids out to the roof of a church building that was underwater, and there they stood. I thought my heart would stop, when I saw where they were. My five- and seven-year-old daughters were standing on the roof surrounded by a thirty-to forty- foot-deep lake. I'm sure nowadays it would have been considered child endangerment, but to Don, it was showing his kids a great time and teaching them not to be afraid of things. It was those special times of family fun and fellowship with other missionaries, which helped us keep our sanity during those long months of language school.

After the first semester, the teacher separated us and put Don in a private class by himself. The Meyers and I continued to be together. Spanish just wouldn't stick in Don's head for some reason or another. He used to talk about it when he was preaching, and he would say, "In order to learn a new language, you need three things: youth—I was forty when I started trying to learn; a good ear for music—I was tone deaf; and a good grasp of the English language—I was in the dumbbell English class all through college."

I used to watch Don prepare a message, and it would amaze me how quickly he could get a wonderful sermon together. I would listen to him answer any Bible question and quote the verse and text where it was found. I would see him add up figures in his head so quickly that it astonished me, but Spanish just knocked him for a loop. Satan was doing the best job he could to knock him out of the running to go to the foreign field. But you see, God had some lessons for Don to learn. When he was on deputation, he had been praised for his preaching and the great job he had done in Long Beach building a strong, soul-winning church. He didn't realize it at the time, but he began to believe it and became pretty proud of the job he had done. Pride was in the way of his being ready to go to the mission field, and God had to bring him down, and that's just what He did.

At the end of eight months, the teacher told Don she felt it would be best if he would just go on to the field and learn the language there. She said she didn't feel as if she could help him anymore, but she thought that once he was on the field, he would be able to learn it fine. She told him it was almost like he had a mental block with Spanish, because he was Mexican and was living in Mexico and couldn't communicate. We hoped that once we were on the field, Don would have to use it every day, and it would stick and everything would then magically come together for him. Years later he would laugh and say, "Guess what—my mental block followed me to Argentina."

I was seven months pregnant and very sick at the time, so we did decide to leave and returned to California. The first Sunday we attended Pastor Thomas Ray's church. He asked Don if he would like to preach that morning. Don looked at him and said, "Brother, I appreciate that you asked me, but no. I just need to listen."

We moved up to Oxnard, California, to wait the arrival of our fifth child. The Fellowship pastor there, Ed Rothenburger, welcomed us to his church and was a tremendous blessing to us during our few months there. But Don was in sad shape. He was depressed and even angry at times. This was an all-time low for him, and a very hard lesson to have to learn. I'm not sure that even he understood at the time what God was trying to teach him. But during the following years when things were going great in the works—and he could have really been proud of what he was accomplishing—he would say, "I don't want another Mexico." I always knew what he meant. Don gave God the honor and glory for what was accomplished under his ministry. He knew that it was by God's wonderful grace. Did the language come magically to him once we were on the field? Not by a long shot. He struggled for many years before it finally began making sense to him.

We spent the next three months trying to recuperate from our time in Mexico—both emotionally and physically. Satan was fighting us with everything he had. Our baby was born with several serious health issues. We sent out a letter to our supporting churches asking for prayer that God would heal her. He gloriously did that, but again, it took a toll on us emotionally. I had a serious heart condition by then, and the doctors were hesitant about letting us leave to go to Argentina. Our documents had not arrived, and Don was scheduled to preach a mission conference in Florida—the week before our departure date from Miami. We decided we would step out by faith and go to Florida—praying that our visas and other documents would arrive there before it was time to leave. Praise God, they did.

Now we were about to face a very difficult trial. That trial was leaving our seventeen-year-old daughter, Donna. She was attending Pacific Coast Baptist Bible College, but we had never been apart more than a couple of weeks. It was hard to say good-bye at the LA airport, and we were not sure when we would see her again. Throughout the years, many people talked about how they had to sacrifice everything to go to the mission field. I feel like this was actually the only sacrifice we ever made in going to Argentina as missionaries.

12

WELCOME TO ARGENTINA

WHEN WE LANDED at the airport in Mendoza, we could see a crowd of people standing on the observation deck. They were holding a sign that said, "Bienvenida a la Argentina, Familia Espinosa." In English it said, "Welcome to Argentina, Espinosa Family." We could hardly believe our eyes. We were all very nervous and excited about arriving, but we had no idea we would receive such a welcome. Missionaries Don and Lucy Nevels brought their whole church out to welcome us to Mendoza.

We had tried to prepare our kids not to be shocked at being kissed on each cheek by those who greeted us, but nothing could have prepared them for the reception we received. Everyone who came greeted each one of us with a kiss on each cheek—men, women, and children. Everyone was laughing and talking, and of course, we could hardly understand anything at all. I began to wonder if we had learned anything in our eight months in Mexico. Their accents were so different from Mexican accents, and even their greeting was different. But one thing was very plain to understand, and that was their joy in having us come to their country.

It took quite a while to get everything through customs, but Brother Nevels took care of all of that for us. We had so much to learn, and we all felt so overwhelmed by the newness of everything. The Nevels loaded us into their car and put our luggage into a covered trailer that actually looked like a covered wagon. After they had settled us in the car, the church people climbed into the trailer and sat on makeshift benches. They were very crowded back there with our luggage, but it didn't seem to bother them at all. What a fun people they were, laughing and joking around with each other. Brother Nevels took us through the back roads, and we went through some very humble neighborhoods. Our kids were all silently looking out the windows at the houses in these neighborhoods, and they looked pretty frightened by it all. Many of the church families lived in those "barrios," as they are called in Argentina. After delivering each family to their home, we finally headed to the Nevels' home. It was very nice and was located in a more upscale neighborhood. The kids began to relax a little bit after we were settled in this missionary's home. I think it began to sink in then that we were really here after two and a half years of deputation and language school.

We began to look for a place to live and found an old house in a beautiful neighborhood. It needed painting and some fixing up.

The owner immediately began to take care of all the changes that needed to be made before we could move into it. We stayed in the Nevels' home for six weeks. We appreciated that they were willing to open up their home to us for such a long period of time. During those six weeks, we began to do all of the paperwork to get permanent resident papers. We had taken all of the required pictures when we were still stateside, but of course, they weren't the pictures that we needed. It seemed like every piece of paperwork that we did had to be redone three or four times. We quickly discovered our frustration threshold. In a foreign country, everything is done differently. That doesn't mean their way was right or wrong, it was just different, and our patience wore pretty thin very quickly. God had many lessons to teach us, especially in patience. This was actually not one of Don's strong points at the time. He always wanted to just jump in with both feet and get it done, but it wasn't quite that easy there. We saw right then that there were going to be many trials up ahead.

We were back together again as a family, and that was a tremendous blessing to this fear-prone missionary wife. I had my "buddy blanket" back, and he could protect me again. Our first real trial began when our crates arrived. We had been used to money trials while living in Long Beach and starting our first church, but this one was different. We were at the mercy of a foreign government that thought all Americans were rich. Praise God we had a rich Father!

Our crates with all of our household goods arrived in Buenos Aires during our fourth week in Argentina. Brother Nevels and Don flew there to do the paperwork to get the crates out of customs and send them to Mendoza. We had been informed that the first time we came into the country, we would be able to get everything in duty-free. We were in for our first real shock and trial. At this time in Argentina, it was very difficult to buy or even find certain basic needs, such as laundry soap, toilet paper, sugar, oil, and many other things. Through the World Vision Organization, the Amway Company furnished missionaries with all of the cleaning products they would need while living in a foreign country for four years at a time. This was a wonderful thing for them to do, but it worked against us getting our crates into the country. When our crates were packed in California, all of the boxes of laundry soap, fabric softener, and other products were all packed on top of the other boxes of household goods. Some were used to fill in spaces so that every inch of the crate was used. When the first crate was opened, there they were! We were labeled "smugglers"! They were just sure we had planned on smuggling in these products and selling them on the black market. Brother Nevels tried to explain, but the lady customs agent was not about to listen to his explanation. She made them open every crate and go through everything in them. There were seven large four-foot by eight-foot crates and five smaller ones. Our appliances were packed individually in the smaller crates. Our "free" customs turned out to be $2,300! We had not planned on this and did not have the money. Praise God, Brother Nevels was able and willing to loan us this amount.

Then the real fun began. The crates had been taken off the ship and loaded on the dock with cranes, but there were no forklifts to get them from the dock to load them in a train car. There were a number of Chilean men looking for work at the docks, so Don and Brother Nevels hired several of these men to load the crates onto the train car. I remember Don laughing and telling about this endeavor. Those crates had to weigh at least a ton each. It was impossible to lift them up. These men somehow concocted a flimsy-looking dolly with some metal bars and wood. How they ever got it to work was a miracle in itself. Don said it was pretty funny watching them do this, but they got it done. Once the crates were loaded on the train, Don and Brother Nevels flew back to

Mendoza and waited for that train to arrive. Upon arrival we had to actually take the crates apart on the train and load everything in Brother Nevels's vehicle and trailer. All of the children helped, along with a few of the church members. It took several trips, but it got done, and at last we were settled into our home and began our life on the mission field.

As soon as we were able to move into our rented home, we hired a language teacher. She came three days a week for two-hour sessions with Don and me and then an hour session with our kids. We spent several hours studying together and then separately, but for Don, the language just wouldn't make any sense. As I stated earlier, we thought once we were on the field and Don would have to use it every day, it would stick. But it didn't! At first he was so busy helping Brother Nevels in the work there in Godoy Cruz that he felt some satisfaction from the fact that he was making a difference and God was using him. Brother Nevels had him preach quite often and teach in the Bible institute but always with Brother Nevels as the interpreter. It was amazing to listen to them. One hardly realized that he was listening to English one minute and Spanish the next. They were an amazing pair, and God blessed them together with souls and growth in Brother Nevels's work. They even preached at youth camps as a pair, and anyone who listened just never thought of them individually.

However, the time came when his lack of the language really hit him. One of those times happened in Chile. The young people of one of the churches invited Don to speak at their "Sweetheart Banquet." They had gone all out for this event with catered food and beautiful decorations, and the young people wore formal attire. Remember, we are talking about a group of very poor young people. It had been a real sacrifice for them to have something this nice. They really hadn't thought about Don not being able to preach in Spanish, because they had always heard him with Brother Nevels.

When Don arrived, he asked the missionary there if he was going to translate the message for him. For some reason the missionary told him no, that he would have to preach it in Spanish himself. Don felt terrible. The banquet was to be held outside on the church patio, which had very poor lighting, and there was no pulpit on which he could lay his Bible or notes. He worked all afternoon trying to write up his notes in Spanish and knew that this was going to be a disaster. He tried so hard, but as he expected, it was a disaster. He knew the young people were very disappointed, and he felt awful about the whole matter. He came home really discouraged.

The final blow came after we had been in Mendoza nearly two years. Brother Nevels was organizing his church, and he had several missionaries present from Chile, Uruguay, and Argentina. All of these men preached in Spanish and did a wonderful job. Some, of course, spoke better than others, but they all could preach in Spanish. This hit Don right between the eyes. I had not seen him so discouraged and even angry since our time in Mexico. It was over the same problem: the language. How could he go out and start a church without being able to speak Spanish? He felt like the biggest dummy in the world, and Satan really did a number on him the last night of the organizational meeting. He came home that night and said, "That's it. I quit! We are leaving here. I'll just pastor in the States, or go to some country where they speak English." I told him that whatever the Lord led him to do, I would be with him. In one of his messages where he was telling about this trial, he said: "I really don't know why we stayed or what God used to speak to me except that I had said so many times to our kids that 'winners never quit and quitters never win' What would it teach our kids if I left now?" Needless to say we stayed, but the language continued to be a real trial of his faith for years.

Our next-door neighbor was a fairly well-to-do lawyer and the head of the sanitation department of the city. He and his wife had nine children, and it worked out that there was one the same age as each of our kids. They became good friends and were a real help to us many times. Having friends their own age helped our kids fit right into the Argentine way of life. While Don and I were still struggling with the language, within six months they were speaking it like their friends. They had absolutely no problem adapting, and that was a tremendous blessing. I loved Mendoza, but I wouldn't go anywhere without Don. There was a large supermarket across town, and for the first few weeks we went there to do our shopping. We were used to shopping for a week or two at a time, so we would take two baskets and fill them up with items. However, when we would go up to the cashier, everyone in the lines around us would just stare and poke each other and snicker.

They always had just a few items in their baskets. Here we were in our bright, plaid, polyester clothing with our baskets full and running over. At first we thought they were laughing about our clothing, but they were staring and laughing at how much we were buying at one time. You see, they would buy for just one meal at a time, which accounted for how few items were in their baskets. Well, after a few weeks of trying to shop this way, we gave in and did it their way. It was just too embarrassing for all of us except Don. Nothing like that ever embarrassed him. Since the supermarket was across town, we started shopping in our own neighborhood. I would send Judy to the meat store and the general store. Shelley would go to the fruit and vegetable market, and John would go to the bread store. They loved it—we are talking about a ten-year-old, an eight-year-old, and a five-year-old. We would buy for only one meal at a time. In the evening they would set out again to do their buying for that meal. I'm ashamed to say that we lived there two years before I even knew one of those store owners. That is how afraid I was to go anywhere without my husband. It was all about speaking Spanish to someone I didn't know.

Remember I mentioned that one of the items not available in the stores was toilet paper? It was very hard to come by, and the rolls were little tiny ones that looked more like crepe paper than toilet paper. Our dear little landlord would try and bring us one roll a week or tell us if any of the stores were going to have it. Can you imagine? One roll a week for six people. One afternoon he came by and told us there was going to be toilet paper at the supermarket on a certain day. We would be able to get one roll per person in the family, but we'd have to be there early, or it would all be gone. So here we were at 7:00 a.m. waiting with over two hundred people for the doors to open at eight o'clock. All of a sudden, the doors were unlocked, and in rushed this horde straight down the center aisle to the toilet paper. It was like a stampede of cattle. We were shoved and pushed and nearly trampled, but we got our six rolls of toilet paper. Even our six-month-old was holding her roll. On the way home, we began to laugh at the comical scenario. Can you imagine two hundred people running down the aisle of a grocery store, pushing and shoving to get a roll of toilet paper? It was serious business! There were many laughs through the years over funny incidents like that one. I think the Lord gives us times in our lives like this so we can look back and not only see the hard trials but the funny things as well. We usually tried to find something to laugh about even in the midst of the storms. **Proverbs 17:22** says, **"A merry heart doeth good like a medicine."** This a wonderful verse, and it soothed over many heartaches.

Soon after we arrived, the peso devaluated, and suddenly we could hardly spend money. Our rent went from a whopping $180 a month to $19 a month. It cost ten cents to take a cab downtown. You could buy a whole cow for about $6. It was incredible. Don used this time to save all he could to be able to have the money with which to start a work. He was able to pay back the loan for our customs charges to Brother Nevels and help with the expenses in the church and the Bible institute. During this time, our mission director came down to visit and took us all out to eat. We had a big steak dinner complete with salad, french fries, coke, and dessert. There were six of us eating, and when the bill came, it was $5.00. The director took the bill and said, "I want to pay for this because I will never have the opportunity to have a bargain like this again."

We ate out as a family a couple times a week and became acquainted with several waiters. These men were incredible with their ability to take everyone's order, never write anything down, and never get it wrong. Don always loved numbers, and this really fascinated him. It also gave him many opportunities to use what little Spanish he knew to witness to these waiters. We saw several of them gloriously saved. Don knew it was of the Lord, because he had to totally depend on Him to help these men understand what he was trying to tell them. Thank God for tracts and for the many times our kids were able to help explain something Don was trying to get across.

When we had been in Mendoza only three months, Don was having some health problems and was experiencing some bleeding. I asked him how bad the pain was, and he laughed and said, "Oh it's nothing big. I probably have cancer and will drop dead from it." I started crying and told him never to talk like that again. Remember this was my "buddy blanket" we were talking about. Besides loving him so much, I was terrified of being away from him. Well, the next day he went out to play a round of golf. He called on the phone and sounded terrible. He told me that he was in the hospital and in terrible pain. Because of his teasing the day before, I thought he was still kidding me. It took several moans and pleading to make me realize that he was really serious. I still had never gone anywhere by myself, and I could not get a hold of the Nevels. I called a cab to take me to the hospital, and en route he tried to dodge a lady walking across the street pushing a baby stroller and ran into the side of a city bus. I was not hurt but terrified. I finally arrived in the "hospital" and was shocked to see where my husband was. He was lying on a narrow gurney in a large room with part of the wall falling down and pieces of the ceiling hanging. I couldn't believe it was really a hospital, let alone a private one. He was in so much pain that he could barely stand it and as yet hadn't received any treatment. They couldn't understand him, and he couldn't understand them. Finally Brother Nevels showed up and explained to the doctor what Don's symptoms were. He then told Don that the doctor thought that he had a urinary tract infection and needed to be hospitalized. They put him in a room with an old man who was in terrible pain himself. The poor man moaned and cried all night. The next morning when I arrived at the hospital, Don had checked himself out. He said that there was no way he would spend another night listening to that. He'd rather go home and die! But of course he didn't die. After a couple of weeks on antibiotics, he was fine, but this problem plagued him off and on for years.

We had been in Argentina about eight or nine months when we decided to go to Chile to attend their youth camp. We hadn't left the city at all except to take a few excursions in the mountains surrounding Mendoza. While we were gone, our house was bombed, and eighteen windows were blown out. In his testimony Don said, "Now they weren't really trying to bomb our house, but we made the mistake of moving next door to a Communist, and the anticommunists were at war with them." They were bombing places all over the country, trying to get rid of the Communists. When we returned home, we couldn't believe our eyes. Our bed was directly below the window in our bedroom, and although there were metal shutters on the windows, there were large jagged pieces of glass stuck in our pillows and all over our room. The blast had blown out all the windows on that side of our house. Our children's rooms were covered with glass. The bomb had gone off at two o'clock in the morning. There's no telling what injuries we would have suffered if we had been home at the time. Other than being out of town, there would have been no other reason not to be at home at this hour. God in His wonderful grace had protected us from this bombing. In one of his testimonies Don laughed and said: *After that incident I felt led by God to move my bed to the other side of the room, and it was a good thing too, because a few months later, they bombed the same house again, and this time blew out eleven windows in our house. The neighbors on the other side of us had just bought a new car, which was parked on the street. The bomb blew out all of the windows and totally demolished that new car. The neighbor was so frustrated that he reached inside the broken car window and locked the door. We watched all of this from our bedroom window. My wife just got the broom and started sweeping up the glass as if it was an everyday occurrence.*

We did praise God that none of our kids were injured, and no one was killed in one of these incidents.

During those years it was actually very dangerous to travel. There would be machine gun nests every few kilometers out on the main highways. We had a pickup with a cover on the back. We had upholstered benches in the back so the kids would be comfortable, but there was actually no way for them to communicate with us when we were on the road. We taught them not to move or open the windows when we were stopped at a checkpoint, for during the military regime, the Communists were attacking the military from the back of pickups. They would lie in the back and rise up with their own machine guns when stopped at checkpoints. We had to trust the Lord to protect our family as we traveled.

Early in our second summer in Mendoza, we went camping in the small town of San Rafael. We had never camped before, but the Nevels had invited us to go with them. I really don't remember exactly when it was, but at the time we still thought we would be staying in Mendoza and starting a work there. As we drove through this beautiful little town, I said to Don, "Maybe the Lord will let us have a mission work here someday. What a beautiful place this is." It was clean and had wide, tree-lined streets and beautiful tile sidewalks that were polished and shining. We drove through it and out to the country to a camping place next to the River Atuel. It was breathtaking. On one side of the river was a mountain of pure multicolored rock, which ended right at the river's edge. The side we camped on was a beautiful forest. We had a great time, and when we left, I really felt as if we had left home. But I didn't say anything more about it. Later on, when we decided to start a work in another city instead of Mendoza, I thought of San Rafael and those feelings I had had earlier in the year. I didn't say anything at the time, though, because I knew that God would lead Don to the place where He would have us go. I'm not saying that Don never asked my input on things, but I trusted him, and I knew that he trusted God to lead us.

We were missing Donna and decided to bring her Argentina for her first two summers in Bible College. We wanted her to see some of Argentina, so we took her to Buenos Aires, and then down the coast of Argentina. Although it was winter time in Argentina, we still had a great time.

I wish I could say that everything was great during our first two years, but Satan always knows our weaknesses and hits us with them when we least expect it. One of Don's weaknesses was his impatience to get things done. He'd see that something could be accomplished in a certain amount of time, but others might not see it that way. The waiting and waiting on things to get done really drove him up the walls sometimes. One such incident occurred when we were looking for the place or city where the Lord would have us start a church. As I mentioned, it had been our original plan to stay in the city of Mendoza and maybe start a work on the other side of town. At the time this town had over a half million people, but God had a different direction for our lives.

There was a couple in the church who had relatives who were believers and lived clear across Argentina in the city of Necochia. They had voiced a desire to have a good Independent Baptist church in their city. This couple from Mendoza was going to visit their relatives and asked Don if he would like to ride along with them. They could introduce him, and he could also "spy out the land," so to speak. It was about a thirteen-hour trip. Don called later that evening, and I could tell he was a little miffed. They were only about two hundred miles away after traveling nearly all day long. They had left about eight o'clock in the morning, and at ten o'clock they stopped by the side of the highway and built a fire to have tea time. After resting for more than an hour, they continued on the journey. They stopped again along the road about 12:30 p.m. They built another fire and cooked their lunch over the open fire. They sat and talked and talked and talked. After they talked, they decided they would take a little siesta. By this time Don was ready to catch a plane. Of course this wasn't an option, because he was out in the middle of the Pampa. After the siesta they started out again about four o'clock, and the car broke down. It was too late to get it fixed that evening, so they stayed in a hotel for the night in a small town out in the middle of nowhere. That was when Don called me. They had been gone all day long and were only two hundred miles away from Mendoza! The couple guaranteed him that they would get him to Necochia the following day. It didn't happen. They finally arrived late the third night.

The next day Don met with the relatives of this couple. They were a sweet Christian family, but really had no desire to commit to being faithful in their service to the Lord or even to a church. Don looked around the city to spy out the land, but he didn't feel this was the place the Lord had for us to start a work. He flew back to Mendoza the next day. He wasn't about to waste another three days getting back home. Looking back at it, he could laugh, but he wasn't laughing at the time. Time was precious to Don, and he had a burden for souls and for finding the place where God would have us start a work.

Shortly after the trip to Necochia, Don was asked to preach in a Bible institute graduation for Missionary John Sawyer in Uruguay. We decided to all go to Buenos Aires first, and from there Don and Missionary Ray Master went to Uruguay to preach in the graduation service. I stayed to help Virginia Masters pack up their house to prepare to go back to the States on their first furlough. After we left Buenos Aires, we went south to Mar del Plata and looked around that city. It was a tourist city of about one hundred and fifty thousand during the winter months but two million during the summer months. Don began to see that during the tourist season people would be so busy attending to the tourists that they would not be interested in the things of God. We left there and started across the Pampa and came to Tres Arroyos. It was another beautiful little city of about one hundred thousand people. We looked around for three days, trying to see if we could find a house for rent and what the possibilities were of renting a space to start a work. Don scouted out the area to see what churches were already there and what the need was for an independent Bible-believing church. There was a small Southern Baptist church that was looking for a pastor, several different branches of Pentecostal churches, a Brethren church, and of course the Catholic churches. There was a definite need there, but in three days of looking, we could not find any houses available to rent or even places to rent to begin a work. We left there a little discouraged, but we knew that God had just the place where He wanted us to be. The last town we visited was San Rafael. We looked around some but couldn't find a house or a place to start a work. Don went to the local newspaper and put an ad in it for a house to rent. Then we received an urgent call from Mendoza to return home, so we headed back. But this time it was different. We knew this was where God wanted us to start a church. He really burdened our hearts for this town. As soon as we returned home, Don put another ad in a newspaper that covered all of the Province of Mendoza.

It was very difficult to rent a house during this time, because there was a law that stated that if you rented your house and the tenants couldn't pay the rent, they could not be evicted. Who would want to rent their houses, not knowing if they would ever receive a penny and be forced to let strangers live there the rest of their lives? It was pretty sad but a reality. Many squatters had settled into vacant houses, and some people who had once rented just stopped paying rent. In the ads Don put in the papers, he said that foreigners from the United States were looking to rent. We received only two calls from those ads. One was a small three-bedroom house that had literally been trashed. There were no light fixtures, no bathroom fixtures, and the ceilings were of cloth and falling down. It was awful. The other house was three kilometers out of town. It was the main house on a large fruit farm and had not been lived in for a long time. But since we were from the United States, the man in charge decided it might be a pretty good bet we would pay the rent. We took the trip to San Rafael to look at it, but it was in pretty bad shape. The man in charge told us that if we wanted it, they would paint it and fix it up. We knew that God had done this for us.

On the day we signed a rental contract, we were in an accident. The owner of the property also owned a large winery. The manager of the winery was in charge of renting the house. We were making a left turn off the main street into the winery (which we found out later was against the law), and a two-trailer fruit truck lost his brakes and hit us broadside on the driver's side. He pushed us sideways for more than a block before he could stop the truck. Miraculously no one was hurt seriously, but our poor truck had major damage. The driver's side was completely smashed in, and the door could not be opened. The window was broken out, and all the trim was torn off. It was pretty banged up. The truck stayed in this condition during our move to San Rafael. It made things difficult but not impossible.

We were excited now. Soon we would be in exactly the place God had prepared for us to serve Him. In one of Don's messages, he stated that he felt one reason God had saved him was because there was a city in Argentina, South America, called San Rafael that needed the Gospel, and God knew that he would be willing to go there and to give the people the Good News of God's plan of salvation.

13

GONE FISHING

After we arrived in Argentina, I found out something about my husband that I hadn't had a clue about until then. I already knew he was the greatest husband and father in the world, but for the first ten years of our marriage, I did not know that Don Espinosa loved to fish. He just never said anything about that part of his life. It may have been because we didn't have the money for him to buy any fishing equipment, or the reason could have been that he was so invested in the ministry in Long Beach and working a secular job to make a living that he never had time for fishing. Whatever the reason was, he never told me.

Needless to say I was a little surprised when we arrived in Argentina, and all of a sudden I was married to a first-class fisherman. In Mendoza, as well as San Rafael, there were lakes and rivers everywhere, all of them full of fish! He especially loved to walk the rivers high up in the Andes Mountains, looking for rainbow trout. When he would find his "glory hole," he would stay there until there were no more bites, and then he would move on to the next one.

I remember on one occasion him finding that perfect spot. He started catching one after another. The kids started chanting "Dale papi, dale papi." (Translation: "Go, Daddy, go.") He then asked the kids and me if we would like to try, and even our two-year-old caught one that day.

When we moved to San Rafael, the fishing was even greater there. Each summer we would take a few days and go camping with our family. We would camp next to a beautiful stream that came out of the side of the mountain. It was about sixty-five miles up into the Andes Mountains from the main highway. John, Shelley, and Anna loved to fish with their dad. I was usually at the campsite with Judy, cooking and reading. It was just a wonderful, relaxing time. I could almost write another book and tell you of all the adventures we had up there. It was a great time together.

Lake Niquil was a large lake only forty-five minutes from our home. Don bought a little boat so he could take me out on the lake to fish. I was "hooked" from that first day out there. It was so peaceful and so much fun pulling out large-mouth bass. Would you believe that the limit was forty fish each per day? During the summer, we would take Mondays off. We'd spend a wonderful day fishing and catch our limit. We would then drive around town and give the fish to the families in the church. It became a Monday night tradition for the families to wait for their portion of the fish that Pastor Espinosa would be bringing to them. It helped them, and we loved doing it. Besides, I was not about to clean eighty bass!

Everyone he ever fished with has a story to tell about their trip. Most of them are pretty funny. However, the one thing they would all tell you was that when Don was fishing, he would do everything he could to catch the next one. He fished for men just like he fished for trout and bass. He would do whatever it took to get that next soul.

14

"FOR IN DUE SEASON WE SHALL REAP IF WE FAINT NOT"

First group of converts to be baptized.

THE FOLLOWING IS an article that Don wrote for the *Baptist Bible Tribune* in 1978 about his struggle with the language and what God was accomplishing despite his lack of mastering the Spanish language. At that time it was the policy of the Baptist Bible Fellowship not to send men over thirty-five to the field, especially if they had to learn a foreign language. Of course that policy has changed drastically.

"God does not make any mistakes." How often have we all said that? When the Lord called me to the field of Argentina I was past the age He calls most to go to the mission field, I answered that call without hesitation, assuredly gathering that the Lord had called me to preach the Gospel there.

When my family and I arrived in Argentina, I was ten to fifteen years older than most missionaries are when they arrive on the field. I was forty years old. It is very difficult for a forty-year-old person to learn a new language. One of my pastor friends from the States visited us and told me that he and some other of my preacher buddies had been discussing my going to the mission field. He told me how they all said, "Espinosa could preach pretty well in English" (his words not mine), and they wondered if I hadn't made a mistake in leaving the States. Nobody but the Lord knows how many millions of times I wanted to give it all up. Or, at least, change to an English-speaking field. Satan has done everything in his power to try and get me off the field of Argentina.

Then in March of last year (1977) we moved to the city of San Rafael to try to begin a new work and establish a Baptist church here in this needy area. It took us nearly two months to find a house to live in, and it took four months more to find a place to hold services. In the meantime I started having services in my home, which was a mile and a half out in the country. I wrote out my lessons and messages and read them. It wasn't much, but it was the best I could do. I just wanted to cry, because I couldn't cut loose and preach the Gospel like I could in English. Did I want to quit? You better believe I did. And if I hadn't preached so many times in English my favorite slogan—"a winner never quits and a quitter never wins"—I believe I would have thrown in the towel. But God's people all over the world were praying for me to get the language. Time after time in my prayer letters to the churches I had requested prayer about my difficulty with the language.

After about three weeks of reading my lessons and messages, I said, "Nuts to this, I'm going to quit this misery and just use a few notes and preach what I know in Spanish, and mistakes or not, I'm going to at least try." And to God be the Glory, it began to come to me. And now just nine months later, by the grace of God, I can teach and preach in Spanish. Oh, I have a long, long way to go, but you don't know the thrill to be able to tell the Good News, and to have these precious people that Christ died for hear and respond to it.

Let me tell you a little of what God has done for us in the short time we have been in the building we found. Being ten to fifteen years late starting, I decided to "go for broke" to see what could be done in this first term, and it was more than half over. So we went all out to fix the building up first-class. I had been able to save some of my work support, and many churches in the States sent in extra to help me with this new church. We spent all of it and then some. But we have a church that can take care of at least four hundred people. Kind of big for the handful of people we had when we moved out of our home into the building. There were about thirty all together. But, oh how God has blessed. In less than three months, there have been eighty-two saved, and we baptized thirty-five. Two of the new Christians have already won others to Christ, and last night in our first all-church visitation we had ten people out calling. We have had a high of one hundred and nine in Sunday school. And to say the least, I am thrilled to death to be serving my wonderful Lord Jesus here in Argentina, South America. Perhaps up there in the States there is a pastor who is thinking, "I'm too old now to go." You can take it from Don Espinosa, it's not easy, but it's well worth it if God calls you. Perhaps somewhere there is another missionary who feels like quitting, ready to throw in the towel. Don't do it. He meant it when He said, "For in due season we shall reap if we faint not" (Galatians 6:9). So keep on keeping on until He comes.

15

OUR MOVE TO SAN RAFAEL

A FEW WEEKS before we moved to San Rafael, we had a pastor friend, Rev. Thomas Ray, visit us from California. He had a wonderful ministry in Huntington Beach and was known for his ability to build a strong Sunday school and church. While he was visiting us in Mendoza, Don asked him to go to San Rafael and "spy" out the land with him. Although Don still could not speak much Spanish, he could introduce himself and give out correspondence courses. They took sixty self-addressed and stamped booklets on Salvation and passed them out in three different neighborhoods: a rich area, a middle-class area, and a very poor area. Every book was graciously received, and Don was really encouraged. A week later we received one of the courses back from a fourteen-year-old boy, Dante Garcia. He had studied the course, filled out the answer page, and mailed it back to us in Mendoza. We sent him the next few courses to work on until we moved to San Rafael.

The following is a newsletter that Don wrote right before we moved, dated March 24, 1977:

There is the old football cheer that says, "Hit them again, harder, harder." As you have been reading in our newsletters, we are about to start a New Testament Baptist Church in San Rafael, Argentina, a city of 150,000 precious souls.

The Mormons are there, as are the Jehovah's Witnesses (now outlawed), the Seventh-day Adventists, the Methodists, the Catholics, and the Pentecostals. As you well know, they aren't winning anyone to Christ. The only chance anyone has of getting saved there is in the Southern Baptist Church. I talked to the pastor, and there is not much happening there. The church is forty-six years old, and he has been pastor for twenty-six years. Last year they baptized four people, and he told me they average about eighty in attendance per Sunday.

Brother, the need is there, and the field is at present wide open. Last month Rev. Thomas Ray visited here from the States. I took him with me to look over the new field and to pass out some literature to see what the reception would be. Would you believe that as we went house to house, we were able to pass out sixty courses on the Bible without one being refused? Brother, these folks are ripe and ready for the Truth. I want to do this thing right, as I'm sure you want me to do. I want to hit this city with everything possible to get the Word of God out, and to start the church in a way that will give us the best chance possible to establish a good, sound work in the two or three years we have before we will have to take a furlough.

When it came to our move from Mendoza to San Rafael, one of my husband's favorite scriptures: "Do all things decently and in order," flew out the window. The value of the dollar was very low, and we couldn't afford to hire a moving company. Unfortunately they didn't have rent-a-truck companies there. We started our move using our pickup truck loaded with the smaller items and boxes. On the first day, we began with things in the storage room. I was helping Don move things around to be able to get boxes out. We had about twenty slabs of plywood that were foot feet by eight feet by

one inch stacked against a wall. All of a sudden they started falling down, and I was standing in front of them. It happened so
quickly that I didn't have time to get out of the way. I fell down,
and they were on top of me. I could feel my left shoulder break,
and the pain was excruciating. By the grace of God, one corner of
the slabs had caught on a small wooden chair, so the whole weight
of the plywood didn't fall on me. Don was scared to death that it
had killed me. I passed out from hitting my head on the concrete
floor. When I came to, Don had lifted the plywood off of me and
was trying to ask me if I was OK. I tried to move and fainted again.
But after coming around again, I was able to sit up and check to
see just what damage was done. There is no 911 emergency there,
and we were entirely on our own at this point. So Don helped me
up, got me into the truck, and took me to an x-ray technician that
we knew. He did some x-rays on me, and all that was broken was
my left shoulder. Talk about a miracle of God's grace. I could have
been injured severely if that small wooden chair had not been in
just the right spot. BUT GOD! That seemed to happen a lot in the
next few years.

Needless to say, from that point on, I wasn't much help to Don
in loading things in the truck. Our kids were all still pretty small,
but they all helped. Don made twenty trips back and forth between
Mendoza and San Rafael, a three-hundred-mile round trip. He
would take one of the kids with him each time, and this became
kind of a ritual between Don and the kids. There was not an exchange house in San Rafael, so after our move, he would have to
make this trip at least once a month to get money exchanged and
do paperwork. He always took one of the kids with him, and they
all looked forward to this special time with their dad. It's funny
how our kids' personalities came out on those trips. Judy would
sleep most of the way, Shelley would be reading her books, John
would play with his soccer and baseball cards, and Anna, who was

two and a half, was always climbing all over him and making him laugh. In 1977, there were no car seats or even seat belts. Sometimes it makes one wonder how we survived everything we went through, but as I said, BUT GOD!

On the last day, we rented a fruit truck and hired four men to help with moving the large furniture and other things. These men assured Don that they had done this many times and knew how to handle the furniture and make sure everything arrived there all right. Never was there a bigger lie told. We just prayed we would have something in one piece left when we got there. Don thought it might be a good idea for me to ride with the driver of the truck. We did not have a lot of confidence in this man by that time. I took Anna and Shelley with me, and the four men rode in the back of this large truck, standing and sitting on our furniture all the way.

Now let's back up a little. Remember that we had already had an accident on the day we signed the rent contract. I had a broken shoulder that was in a sling this whole time, we had no one to help us make this move, and we had already made twenty roundtrips in our pickup. Don had unloaded most of our smaller things in the living room and dining room area, so things were piled pretty high already. We also had the young Uruguayan couple supposedly arriving that evening by train in San Rafael. There definitely was a lot going on at the time.

Now let's get back to the trip. Don followed in the pickup. I should have noticed when I climbed in the truck that there was a jug of wine on the floor, but Shelley and Anna had climbed in first and I just didn't notice it. We had just left the city limits when out came that jug. The driver began to drink from it and drank the whole way. I was already an emotional basket case from all that had happened, and I was scared to death. I tried to signal Don through the window, but he didn't see it. By the

grace of God, we arrived in San Rafael in one piece. As we pulled
into the circle drive that was in front of the house, a tree branch
caught on our king-size mattress and ripped it right down the
side. Don could see this was about to happen and tried to signal
the driver to stop, but he didn't stop, and the damage was done.
When we climbed out of the truck, I was already about in tears,
but then they started carrying our furniture into the house. Our
couch was torn in the back, our beautiful upright piano was terribly scratched, the vinyl on the top of Don's desk was torn, and
the kitchen stove was dented in where a man had stood on it
all the way. I was just heartsick, but at least we had arrived in
one piece. The big surprise came when we entered the house.
The Uruguayan couple had arrived that morning, and there they
stood with their bags and two little girls.

Now here was another problem, for the older girl, who was two
years old, was holding Anna's favorite "Mrs. Beasley doll." World
War III began to take place right there in the entrance. Anna, who
was also two years old, tried to take her doll out of the arms of the
other little girl, who was not about to let go of it. They both began to scream and pull on poor Mrs. Beasley. Anna had cried and
cried when she had found out that her Mrs. Beasley was gone a few
days before, and then to walk into a new place and see her favorite
doll in someone else's arms was just too much. For the next three
days, all we heard was "Es mia; no es mia." Translation of that isn't
too difficult—"It's mine; no, it's mine!"

As they continued bringing the furniture in, we saw that
everything was damaged. I wanted to cry but didn't feel as if it
would be a good testimony. I just kept thinking, "It's just material
things," but it did hurt. To top everything off, nothing would fit
where it was supposed to go or just didn't work when we put it
into place. Off the sun porch was a door that led to a dirt cellar.
The previous tenants had used this to store their home-canned

goods. I went down there to see it that first day. That was a big mistake. Before we moved into the house, the bugs and mice had had the run of the place, and now they were all in the cellar. The second I stepped off the last step, which was actually not much more than a ladder, a mouse ran across my feet. Now I've never had a good relationship with mice or spiders, and this was not a good way to start off our new life in San Rafael. I screamed and actually made it up the stairs faster than I had gone down. I quickly shut the door and vowed not to go down there again until it had been fumigated.

Three days later after we moved in and after many, many hours of unpacking and trying to make a home out of this house, I had a terrible nightmare. Now this was not a frequent happening, so it scared my poor husband to death. He said that I screamed really loud and sat straight up in the bed. I looked at him and said, "You have to get me out of here now. There are spiders and mice all over me." He said he was ready to pack the bags and get me out of there, but then I woke up. I looked at him and asked what had happened. After he told me what I said, I looked at him again and told him that after all we had been through, no mice or spiders were going to keep us from doing God's will. This was actually the beginning of many mice and spiders, so to speak. The trials and challenges that we had to go through were incredible, but so was God's grace that took us through every one of them.

Anna came down with an ear infection that first week, and Don set out to find a doctor who could speak English. He went to a large pharmacy, and they somehow understood that he was looking for a doctor who spoke English. They called a pediatrician, Dr. Florentina Ponce, and she told Don to bring Anna to her house, which was also her office. This began a twenty-seven-year friendship with a dear, precious lady. She had just returned to Argentina after studying in Charlotte, North Carolina. Although she was a very staunch Catholic, she did everything she could to help us. She directed us to a man named Sr. Olive who fixed all the appliances. He came out to the house and after several days had everything up and running. He could make whatever part necessary to fix an American appliance. He was an amazing man and a real help to us. And so began our life in San Rafael.

16

GLAD THAT ONE'S OVER

AFTER GOING THROUGH a serious trial, Don would always say, "Glad that one's over." He'd tell us this and assure us that whatever came next wouldn't be a surprise to the Lord either. God's grace would be sufficient to take us through it. It's funny how we expect our kids to experience the same faith in our Lord as we as parents do, but they have to learn and experience it for themselves. Thinking back over our trials and what our kids went through, it's no wonder they have had to learn for themselves how to trust God. But, one thing they never had to wonder about was their dad's reaction to those trials. He totally trusted God to lead and direct him and to give him the grace to lead his family through the hard times.

Because of time and space, there is no way I could write about all the trials we went through It would take several volumes to cover all God so graciously brought us through and how this tremendous man of God managed to always thank Him not only for the blessings in our lives but also the hard times. Years ago we talked about writing all these things down, but Don laughed and said that it would have to be called "Espinosa's Believe or Not!" It really would be hard for people to believe it.

The first few years on the field were during a very unstable political time. While we lived in Mendoza, we heard of many people being kidnapped and never seen again. A church member's neighbor was kidnapped. He was one of the few to be returned home but in a pine box. He had been tortured and severely beaten, and all of his fingernails and toenails had been pulled out. He had cigarette burns all over his body. He was then shot in the back of the head.

Usually it happened like this: a Ford Falcon would drive up in front of the home of someone they suspected of being a terrorist. There would be four men dressed like policemen. They had machine guns and would arrive with their guns pointed out of the windows at the person's home. Two of them would get out of the car and go up and knock on the door. They would tell the man or woman he or she had ten minutes to get dressed and come with them. It almost always happened early in the morning. They would leave, and the family would never hear from them again. They were kidnapping rich men and foreigners and holding them for ransom, but they always killed them in the end. They also kidnapped anyone that they thought might have connections with terrorist groups. They were usually young couples with families. The men would take the whole family, kill the parents, and give the children to army officials to raise as their own. Not until many years later did all of this come to light. When all of this was discovered, many of the children were reunited with their grandparents, but by this time they were grown and considered the military families their real families.

A few weeks after moving to San Rafael, we heard a car drive up our circle drive and park in front of our house at 6:30 in the morning. We lived out in the country and didn't have a phone.

Back then there were no cell phones either. Don got up and looked out the window, and sure enough there was a Ford Falcon with four machines guns pointing out the windows. Two of the men got out, and they were dressed like policemen. This didn't mean that they were the police or that we would be safe with them. They rang the doorbell, and Don went to answer it. They told him that he had ten minutes to get dressed and come with them. Don had me write down all the numbers of his documents, Argentine as well as his American passport. We knelt down and prayed that God would protect him and bring him back home safely. However, the honest truth was that we really believed we would never see each other again. He told me if he wasn't back in an hour to go into the city and call the American embassy in Buenos Aires and also the missionaries there. We didn't wake the kids up, because we didn't want to scare them. I just knelt and prayed and prayed that God would protect him. As they left he began to pray that if he had to die, that he would die like a man and not defile the name of His Lord. He said when they turned toward town, he felt a little better and thought they might really be police, but being in police custody could sometimes be as bad as being in the company of the ones pretending to be policemen. When they arrived at the police station, they began to explain why he had been arrested.

We had rented an apartment for the young Uruguayan couple who had come to work with us, but they couldn't get their papers in order and had returned to Uruguay. Since the rent was very cheap and we had used one large room as storage for Bibles, correspondence courses, other printed materials, and our printing press, we decided to keep on renting the apartment until our rent contract was up. At the time, the Jehovah Witnesses had been prohibited from practicing their religion, and police thought with those materials and the printing press that we were doing something illegal. Praise God that Don had registered everything with the government when we arrived in San Rafael. He had the papers with him proving that we had permission to have the printing press and that we were Baptists and not Jehovah Witnesses. There were still some other matters to clear up, but he asked them to please take him home so he could let me know that he was all right. When he walked in, we both began to cry and pray and thank God that he was safe. He used to laugh and say, "And you wonder why I have gray hair?"

Little did we know that some of our biggest trials were yet to come.

17

TO GAIN THE MORE

I COR. 9:19, 22: "For though I be free from all men, yet have I made myself servant unto all, that I might gain the more...To the weak became I as weak, that I might gain the weak: I am made all things to all men, that I might by all means save some."

DON LOVED SOULS and did everything he could to win them to Christ. His ministry was based on these two scriptures.

I mentioned before that we moved into our home on Saturday. Sunday morning we decided to have a Bible study with the Rosado family from Uruguay. We also invited the caretaker and his family to join us.

During the next week, Don and Miguel Rosado went to visit Dante. He was from the middle-class neighborhood. His mother very graciously invited them in to talk. Her father had been a Pentecostal pastor, and she had received the Lord as a young girl, but she had not been to church for more than twenty-five years. Don invited them to come the following Sunday to meet with us for a Bible study and preaching. Don told them that he would pick them up if they would like to come.

Don had to make a trip back to Mendoza that week to get some body work done on the pickup truck. The body shop man told him that he had a car he would loan us while they fixed our truck. It was a twenty-five-year-old Jeep with no windows. It was the first part of winter by then and very cold, but Don really didn't have a choice, so he took it. We put plastic on the window frames to keep out the cold and wind.

Sunday morning he went to pick up Dante and his mother, but only Dante came. We had a pastor friend, Rev. Harold Ramsey, come down to visit all of the missionaries that his church support- ed in Chile, Argentina, and Uruguay. He just happened to be visit- ing us that week of our very first service in San Rafael. There were sixteen in the service: the caretaker and his family, the Rosados, Dante, Pastor Ramsey, and our family. Dante received Christ as his Savior that morning. He didn't understand much that Don preached, but he did understand the scriptures that were read. This young man was gloriously saved, and from that day on, his life was changed. Don always said, "I found my Timothy in the ministry that first Sunday." I will tell you more about him later. His mother came the following week and was faithful to the Lord until the day she went home to be with Him.

The caretaker, Benjamin Olivares, asked us if we would visit his relatives who lived in a small village eighteen miles away. We drove to the village, Venticinco de Mayo, in this jeep to visit the family. There were four adults and two teenagers at home that evening. They patiently listened to our poor Spanish, but seemed to un- derstand the scriptures that Don showed them on how to receive Christ as their Savior. All six made a profession of faith that night. One thing we had not understood at the time was the reason the caretaker wanted us to visit his relatives. He had told Don that he wanted his family to receive the "suerte" that he had received since we moved into the house. Don did not understand the word *suerte*. It means good luck or good fortune. We hired his wife to help us in the house, and things were looking up financially for them. His relatives were in a very bad situation at that time. His uncle was about to be sent to jail for not paying his bills, and none of the men in the family had jobs. His uncle was a drunk and couldn't keep a job. The very next week after making a profession of faith, Brother Olivarez and his oldest son both found work. He stopped drinking and for the first time in many years was sober. He had truly received *suerte*. However, the truth was that he and his wife had really accepted Christ as their Savior.

She was the matriarch of the family, and in Argentina that is a very important and influential position. Mrs. Olivarez was a dear, faithful saint of God until she went to Heaven nearly twenty-five years later. Although the others in their family made professions of faith and came for several months, when difficulties or worldly pleasures came along, they dropped out one by one. A couple of weeks after the Olivarez received the Lord, Gogue, their only daughter, received Christ, and she is still faithfully serving the Lord. Don drove the eighteen miles eight times a week for several months to pick them up for all of the services and to visit them on Thursday nights to teach them the basic Bible doctrines. During that time, Elsa Olivarez, the caretaker's wife, asked us to visit her sister in San Rafael. She and four of her children made professions of faith and began to come to the services in our home. Her husband was an alcoholic but came once in a while. He made a profession of faith but never actually received Christ as his Savior. By this time we had our truck, and Don would make a couple of trips for each service to bring the people to our home.

Don invited Mr. Olive, the fix-it man, to come visit the services. He came and was saved during those first couple of weeks. We visited him and his family every week for months, but he was the only one who received Christ as his Savior. His wife was very nice to us and always treated us with respect, but she was very Catholic and would not come to our services. Don witnessed to her every week, and she always listened as he taught her husband the truths of God's Word, but she would not make a profession of faith.

We began looking for a building to hold services in right from our first week in San Rafael. After a couple months, we found a large warehouse on the main street, just three blocks from the center of town. The location was perfect and was directly in front of one of the major clinics in the town. We had to have someone to be a cosigner in order to rent it. Although she was Catholic, Dr. Florentina Ponce did this wonderful thing for us. We had saved up over $5000 during our time in Mendoza, and we used this money to fix up the warehouse. We made an auditorium that would comfortably seat two hundred and three classrooms and two bathrooms. It was a wonderful, exciting time not only for us, but also for those who had been saved and had been attending the services in our home. We were consistently running twenty-five or more in the house.

Brother Olive became Don's right-hand man and helped him employ all the builders and workmen. He was so happy doing this, and Don really depended on him and appreciated what he was doing. He'd take time off from his own home business to help Don in whatever way he could. It took us five months to get the building ready, but Don had done it first-class. He felt that God deserved the best we could do for Him. All of the Catholic churches were very beautiful, and he felt that God shouldn't receive any less from His children. He had padded benches made, built a platform and finished it with a beautiful rock finish, built a baptistery under the platform, and had beautiful wood-and-glass doors made for the auditorium. We all worked together to paint and fix up the classrooms and the bathrooms. It was such a joy to watch these new Christians working together and loving each other in spite of the class differences between them. About half of the people were middle-class, and the other half were very poor people. It's amazing how the love of Christ changed their outlook. Class difference is very prevalent in Argentina, but among these Christians, it hardly existed.

While the construction was in progress, our daughter, Judy, and I wrote over five hundred letters on our old flex writer. We sent these letters to all of the business people in San Rafael. We went door to door passing out invitations for the first service, along with Gospel tracts. Don put announcements on the radio about the new church opening up. He had invited Missionary Walter Silva from Uruguay to preach an eight-day meeting to inaugurate the beginning of the services held in the building. We were excited to see what God was going to do for us in that first Sunday-morning service.

Until this time we had not had a baptismal service for those who had been saved and attending the services in our home. Don decided to wait until the last Sunday night of the meeting to have our first baptism. He taught the meaning of baptism and what it represented and said that it was the next step of obedience in their Christian lives. He gave an invitation the last Sunday morning that we met in our home, and nearly everyone presented themselves for baptism—everyone except the daughter of Mr. and Mrs. Olivarez, who stopped us cold with a question that morning. She said, "How do we know that you are not deceiving us as the Catholic Church has?" After all those months of faithfully bringing them to the services and preaching and teaching them, she still had that doubt. It really knocked me for a loop, but Don just patiently explained to her from the scriptures how she could know and understand if we were telling her the truth or not. He always told his congregation to test everything he preached by the Word of God. Praise God she was among those who were baptized in that first baptismal service.

After five months of preparation and a lot of hard work, God gave us a great service on Sunday morning. There were five people representing different businesses in town, and Dr. Florentina Ponce came with her father. There were a few other visitors in addition to those who had been meeting in our home. It was a wonderful service, and Don was happy with the results. During the week we had visitors every night, and many were saved. On the following Sunday night, we had our first baptismal service with twenty-eight following the Lord in baptism. Dr. Ponce's father came every night and wanted to get baptized, but his wife and Dr. Ponce's sister put a quick stop to that. He no longer was able to attend any of the services, but we believe that he really accepted Christ as his Savior and is in heaven today.

We had many new contacts to visit and felt as if things were really going to progress. Don was somewhat concerned that after hearing Pastor Silva preach for eight days, those new converts would be disappointed when he started preaching using his limited Spanish. However, Don knew that if he didn't preach and teach them the Word of God, they would not hear it anywhere else. There were many times when Don wanted to throw in the towel, so to speak, concerning his Spanish, but he always tried to improve. He would laugh at his mistakes and try to learn from them. He made funny mistakes and sometimes embarrassing ones. We all did. However, one of the funniest ones came to light nearly five years after we had been in San Rafael. We were in Denver, Colorado, on a short furlough when we received a cassette tape from some of our young people in San Rafael. After greeting us and telling us about the things that were happening there, one of the young men said, "Pastor, we hope that you have learned the difference between the devil and the fork by now." That doesn't sound very funny in English, but Don had preached a whole message confusing the Spanish words *tentador* and *tenedor*. *Tentador* is the tempter, or the devil. *Tenedor* is a fork. He laughed and said, "Can you believe that I preached a whole message telling them that they better be careful, because the fork was after them?" On another occasion a lady came back on Sunday night and told Don that on the way home she had finally figured out what he was trying to tell them.

Years later Dante and his wife, Jovita, were laughing with us over some of our mistakes, and Dante said, "When I got saved, I really didn't understand anything that Pastor Espinosa was saying, but I did understand the scriptures that he read." Jovita, who was saved two years later, told us that she didn't understand what he was saying either when he was preaching, but she understood the scriptures. Any time we seemed to think we were doing a pretty good job, God had a way to bring us to our knees and humble us. Don always gave God the honor and glory for any of the success of his ministry, because without Him, nothing would have been accomplished. Don had been a romping, stomping, shouting preacher in Long Beach; here he was now, struggling to get the simple messages across. Sometimes he'd tell me that he wished he could just let go and preach as he did in English. It was a very difficult struggle for him.

As the years went on, he began to really enjoy preaching again. He was concerned about his mistakes, but he no longer held back anything when he preached. From that very first service in the new facilities, we had people saved each week. Don was encouraged about the results and the way God was blessing, despite his poor Spanish.

Dante Garcia, Don's "Timothy in the Lord," was a tremendous blessing to us. When Dante got saved, he was a semipro soccer player. He played on the city's top team and was being wooed by one of the major teams in the country. He was that good. Don used to say, "Dante didn't run across the field, he glided across it." He was amazing to watch, and he was the hope of his family for their future. He was also a very intelligent young man. He made excellent grades in school and had a bright future ahead of him, but he saw right from the beginning that his soccer life and his Christian life were going to collide. The games were on weekends, usually Sundays, and his practice was on Wednesday nights. We didn't say anything to him about the conflict, but he saw it right away. He came to Don and asked his advice. Dante told Don he knew his father would be very angry if he quit soccer, but he felt in his heart that it was what the Lord was asking of him. What a tremendous young man he was then, and what a tremendous man of God he is now. Dante did quit soccer, and his dad was very, very angry about it. He would not come to church for a long time, but then God began to soften his heart. Dante grew from the moment he received Christ as his Savior, and he never faltered. There was no guile in him at all. Don used to call him "the world's smallest giant" because he is just five feet tall. Don started the Bible institute the following year, and of course, Dante was the first to sign up to attend. He was fifteen years old. After Don taught his students homiletics, he would have the students preach short messages to practice. After listening to Dante's first ten-minute message, Don knew that God had called Dante to preach the Word of God. He asked Dante to preach one Sunday night. Dante was a little worried the congregation would not be able to see him behind the pulpit because he was so short. When he stood up to preach, he grew about six inches. Don wondered what he was standing on. When Dante gave the invitation, twelve people made professions of faith that night. After the service Don looked behind the pulpit to see how Dante had grown those six inches. He had gone to the nursery and borrowed one of the potty chairs. God had His hand on this young man's life. Later I will share more about Dante and his ministry and the huge part he played in our lives and in Don's ministry.

18

"ALL THINGS TO ALL MEN THAT I MIGHT BY ALL MEANS SAVE SOME"
I COR. 9:22B

FROM THE BEGINNING of the ministry in San Rafael, Don tried to put in practice the things he had learned and used in Long Beach. We sent out letters to each visitor present at the services and letters to new converts. We would visit each new visitor and follow up on each person saved. We gave them a Bible and the first course of a Bible study to help them get started out right. We started out with visitation on Thursday nights, going door-to-door and giving out tracts and invitations to come to the services. We started printing up a weekly bulletin with all the coming events listed. We sent the bulletin to all of our prospects each week. We encouraged the new converts to pass out tracts and invite all of their friends and relatives. We had Sunday school campaigns and big Sundays with special events. Don's favorite was the apple orchard campaign. Since he was saved because of it, it was the first one that he tried. He used Bibles and Bible study help books as prizes for these campaigns. He used everything that he had learned at Jack Hyles's Pastor School. We were averaging in the high sixties and had hit a hundred a couple of times, but it seemed that we just stayed at that point and couldn't get over that one-hundred mark.

In June 1978, I had to make a trip back to the States to have major surgery. While I was there, Don heard of a movie that was being shown in Mexico. Many souls were being saved through it. He asked me to try to locate it and see if we could buy or rent a copy of it. Also, we needed a movie projector. So, while recuperating from my surgery, I began to make the calls to track down this film. After trying for six weeks, I finally found it and made arrangements to rent it for a year. One of our supporting churches bought us the projector. They both arrived the day before I was supposed to fly back to Argentina. Satan definitely did not want me to take this film to Argentina, but praise God, He won the victory. The film was *The Burning Hell* by Estes Perkell from Mississippi. Don announced on the air that we were showing this film Friday night at the church. We only had one major radio station and one TV station, so everyone heard the announcements.

That first Friday night, the church was full and fourteen were saved. We gave them the first lesson of the correspondence course, a copy of John and Romans, and an invitation to come back on Sunday. Everyone there received a printed invitation to come the next Sunday, and we had over eighty in attendance. The next Friday night we had another full house, and nineteen were saved. Don decided to show the film twice on Friday nights and twice on Saturday nights. He kept the announcements on the radio and TV. We had fifty-three saved that weekend and eleven saved on Sunday. The following week we had forty-six saved from the film and eighteen saved on Sunday. Two Catholic priests came dressed in plain clothes, but the young people who had recently been saved recognized them. The priests spoke on TV the next week and denounced us as liars, saying there was no way we could know for sure that people would not have to go to hell. They literally forbade the Catholic people to see this film. It worked in reverse. People wanted to see what these Catholic priests were so upset about.

In September we had another revival meeting with Missionary Walter Silva and showed the film on Sunday night. There were ninety saved during the week and twenty-five on Sunday. All of the young people were doing the correspondence courses; at one time we had seventy-six enrolled. Every service they would bring back a booklet and were ready for another one. They were excited and eager to learn, but most of the excitement was about a chart we made with all of the courses listed and the names of those who were working on each course. When they finished one lesson, they would receive a star by their name. Each service they came with their lesson finished, ready for the next lesson. We later found out that large groups were meeting together and copying each other's books. It was all about getting the stars by their names. We figured that it was still worth it, because they were doing them and learning something.

It didn't take us long to figure out who were the leaders of each group of kids. We could tell that one of the young men from a rough neighborhood was a natural leader. His name was Luis Yañez. But there was another reason that he really stood out. He had thick, black hair that hung down to his shoulders. He wore a jean jacket with the sleeves torn out over a T-shirt and tight blue jeans. For the first couple of weeks, he came dressed like this, but one Sunday he came, and he had cut his hair a little bit. Each Sunday he would come, and it would be a little shorter. It became a topic of conversation each week. It was funny, and we laughed about it many times through the years, but with each haircut came a young man a little more serious about serving the Lord. He start-ed dressing in a shirt and tie, and the change in him was incred-ible. He came that first night with his girlfriend, Sara, and her sisters. They were all saved at the same time. Sara was timid and very quiet and was so different from him. They came faithfully and very seldom missed a service. Luis began to really grow from the first week that he was saved. He was a construction worker and began helping with projects around the church. He loved working and was very good at what he did. He was always ready to help with whatever needed to be done. He is now pastor of Temple Baptist Church of San Rafael. We will be sharing more about his life as we talk about the progress of the work in San Rafael.

But all was not perfect with this group. I wish I could say that they all grew and became strong, Christian young people, but sad-ly that was not the case with many of them. These kids came from very rough neighborhoods and backgrounds. Don had to break up more than one fight out behind the church. One young man was a boxer, and he just couldn't seem to keep his talents in the boxing ring. He came for several months, but sad to say the attractions of the world drew him back into his old life. There were several like this: they had one foot in the church, but wanted to keep the other in the world.

We had young girls who were already pregnant when they received Christ, and several were single moms. We encouraged them to continue coming to church and to raise their little ones for Christ. Some did, and others dropped by the wayside. Don preached from the Word of God on the sin of fornication, and on purity, and on how to resist Satan's temptations. He tried to show them the consequences of their sin, but many would not listen and continued to live as they did before making a profession of faith. Soon they stopped coming. It was heartbreaking to see this, but it had been their way of life for as long as anyone could remember.

We had one young lady in particular who seemed to soak up the Word of God and had such potential of serving the Lord. She had such a sweet, humble spirit, but Satan tripped her up along the way. She was a very homely girl and felt that she would always remain single. But Satan used a handsome young man from her neighborhood to entice her into sin. A few weeks later, she dropped out of church. We went to visit her, and at first she wouldn't come out to see us. She was ashamed. We tried to help her, but she just couldn't face the consequences of her sin. Later that young man married her, and they had four children together. But at the same time, he fathered other children with other young girls. It was so sad to see these young people destroying their lives and bringing children into this type of environment. One blessing is that some of this man's children from two different families are now saved and have taken an active part in the church.

Another young woman came a couple of times but did not make a profession of faith. It seemed Satan was winning many victories, but then so was the Lord. In 1980 this young lady, who had visited two years before, came back, and this time she received Christ as her Savior. Her name was Norma Fuentes. Her younger sister, Jovita, came to see the film and was saved. She invited Norma to come with her.

Norma was now married and had a little boy. Norma and Jovita began to come to every service, and they grew in the Lord by leaps and bounds. But Norma's husband, who had also visited once or twice before, wanted nothing to do with the Lord or anything concerning Him. He and his family began to ridicule Norma and made life very difficult for her. Their marriage was a disaster at this point. He finally gave her an ultimatum. She could keep coming to church if she wanted to, but she had to be home on Sunday by noon with his dinner on the table. She was really going through the fires, but God was preparing her for great things up ahead.

She came to us and asked what she should do. We told her that she had to obey her husband and then maybe she would be able to win him with her testimony. So she would come to the service but would leave in time to be home and have the food on the table at noon. This went on for months, and by this time she had had another little boy. Carlos became more and more belligerent and was ready to leave his family. Divorce was against the law, but separating was still very devastating. One Sunday morning Carlos came to church. It was March 31, 1985, and the day we broke ground for our new church building. Carlos received Christ that morning and was gloriously saved. His spiritual birthday is written on the cornerstone of Templo Bautista de San Rafael.

Like Luis and Dante, Carlos began to immediately grow in Christ. He was a clean-cut-looking young man, but he had a lot of vices to give up, and thankfully he did. This young man, who made life miserable for his wife and family before he accepted Christ, is now the pastor of Bible Baptist Church of Bowen, Argentina. His two little boys have married wonderful Christian girls and are serving the Lord. One is the junior boy teacher, Awana club leader, and a member of the choir at Temple Baptist Church in San Rafael. His other son, Damian, worked with Missionary Joe Merlo in Southern Argentina for several months and is now the pastor of Brother Merlo's church while he is in the States on furlough. Carlos's daughter, Ruth, has graduated from Bible College and is now married to a young preacher boy. They are working in Rosario with a missionary. God has really blessed Norma's willingness to do His will so many years ago. She is a wonderful helpmeet for her husband, Carlos.

In 1979 we took a short furlough. Missionary Jim Strickland came and watched over the work for the few months we were gone. The church did well under Brother Strickland's leadership, but we were anxious to return and continue our work there in San Rafael.

The following newsletter tells of a new ministry that God laid on Don's heart before taking that short furlough and how God supplied the needs to do this ministry. From the newsletter dated May 1980:

"WE KNOW THAT GOD LOVES THE SHEPHERDS"

In Luke chapter two we read how the shepherds were the first to hear the "good tidings of great joy" that the Savior had been born. So we know that God is interested even in the lowly shepherds. Here in Argentina, where we live, there are hundreds of shepherds in the high Andes Mountains and also in the foothills of the Andes. Before we left last July for a short furlough, it had really been on my heart to try to reach these people with the Gospel, these people who God loves very much. The problem, you see, is that most all of them cannot read and they do not have electricity. Passing out tracts and Bibles would not have done any good since they could not read. We do not have a generator so we can't gather crowds of people up there to show the Gospel films to try to win them to Christ. But God knew all about this!

While on furlough I ran across God's way of reaching these people with Gospel recordings. But without electricity????? Yes, without electricity. Gospel Recordings of Glendale, California, supplied me with five hundred "card talks." These are cardboard apparatus that play records of the Gospel by turning the records with a ballpoint pen or even a sharp stick. They also gave me 1,500 records to go along with the "card talks." So when my crates finally arrived last week with these records, I gathered up some of our preacher boys and headed for the mountains with the "good tidings of great joy" that the Savior had been born. We left early in the morning and didn't get back until late at night. During all this time we were only able to visit seventeen homes, because they are so spread out.

The people were really happy to see us and gladly received the records and the record players. At first nearly all of them were suspicious of us. They couldn't believe we had come all that way to give them something for free. But after we talked to them for a while, they warmed up to us and were very grateful for the Word of God. When we returned home that night, we were all rejoicing in the Lord, because we knew that people who had never heard the Word of God were now listening to the way of salvation. So the precious seed has been sown. Please pray that it will bring forth fruit as the Lord has promised that it would.

As we went back up in the mountains years later, we found that many still had the record players and still played them often. We passed out nearly all five hundred of them plus another fifty Japanese-language ones that were mistakenly put in our crates. You see, there is a Japanese colony just over fifty miles from San Rafael. Was it a mistake or God's leading that the box of Japanese language records had been put in our crates?

God blessed this ministry, and many of those shepherds came to know the Lord. Many attend monthly services held by Pastor Dante Garcia high up in the Andes Mountains. This has been one of Pastor Garcia's favorite ministries through the years.

After all the trips up and down those dirt mountain roads, the motor in our truck was pretty shot. We needed a new engine, body work, new seats, and a number of other things fixed. Don checked into the prices of getting the work done in Mendoza and in San Rafael. He always shopped for the best price. About this same time, Missionary Walter Silva had invited Don to preach a meeting for him in Uruguay. Don learned from a missionary friend in Brazil that he could get the truck fixed there for one-third of the price it would cost in Argentina. We decided to drive to Brazil (praying the whole way that the truck would get us there), leave the truck there in Porte Allegre, and take a bus to Montevideo, Uruguay, to preach the meeting. This trip was one of the most memorable trips we ever made with our family.

We had a wonderful time in Montevideo with the Silvas, and God blessed the revival meeting with souls being saved. Then the fun began with our return trip to Porte Allegre, Brazil. After picking up the almost like-new truck, we went shopping and bought a few things, which were so much cheaper there than at home. The kids were happy with their new things and in high spirits. Don wanted to cross over into Argentina later in the evening so it wouldn't be so noticeable that the truck had been repaired and refurbished. He wasn't being sneaky, just trying to use a little wisdom!

We made a bed in the back where the kids could sleep, because we wanted to go as far as we could before stopping for the night. We were going to fill up the truck with gas right before we crossed the border, because it was so much cheaper in Brazil. What we did not know was the gas stations closed early in the evening on Fridays and didn't open again until Sunday. We had no choice but to cross the border into Argentina, stay in a hotel there, and get gas for the rest of the trip in the morning. We drove to the nearest town, and the one hotel there was very expensive. We looked around and found a boarding house that was a little less expensive. By now it was two o'clock in the morning. We walked into the only room they had available and couldn't believe our eyes.

The room was very long and narrow with seven small twin beds all in a row. The kids looked at it and began to laugh. I said it looked like Snow White and the seven dwarves lived there. Everyone started laughing, and Shelley, our fourteen-year-old, said it looked more like the typhoid fever ward in the Florence Nightingale movie. By then we were all laughing hysterically. Besides being very narrow, it had only one twenty-five-watt light bulb hanging on a wire in the middle of the room. There was no lock on the door, and the only other furniture was a dilapidated old table. The walls were paper-thin, so Don was trying to calm the kids down. We pushed the table in front of the door and sat all of our suitcases on top of it. There was water and mildew on the walls, and the bathroom was worse yet. But no one complained. Finally, everyone was in bed but me. Then John found a cigarette lighter in his bed, and the laughter started again. I finally turned the light out and lay down in my bed. When I tried to pull the sheet up, it ripped right down the middle. As you can imagine, everyone lost it then. We were so grateful our kids were able to just laugh and roll with the punches. They were great kids and adapted to anything. The funny thing about it was that we had stayed in a Hilton Suites Hotel in the States for less money than we paid for the room that night. However, looking at the good side of it, we didn't have to pay customs for the newly overhauled motor God so graciously supplied for us. This was just one of the fun times we had as a family. There were many trials, but also a lot of laughter. It seemed to be the way that we dealt with the problems that came along.

Upon returning to San Rafael, we started another new ministry of going out to the small villages around us and showing the Gospel films. We would have crowds up to four hundred people gathered to see the films. Many professions of faith were made, and we would pass out Gospels of John, the book of Romans, and the first lesson of correspondence course. Many of these people did the complete correspondence courses through the following months. We were also having folks saved in nearly every service in church. We passed out ten thousand Gospels of John door to door in San Rafael. At this time the church people had knocked on over two thousand doors and the people had received the tracts gladly. Our Bible institute had ten students, and the church was excited about what was happening in our town. In a newsletter dated June 8, 1980, Don reported that two-hundred-fifty-two souls had been saved during that year so far.

In December 1980 we organized our first church as missionaries: Templo Bautista de San Rafael was now a church instead of a mission. Our attendance was averaging around one hundred and twenty by then, and people were seeing the fruits of their labor.

We also started a mission church in Las Heras, Mendoza, that year. One of the preacher boys came to Don with a burden for that city. It is a small town with mostly lower-middle-class people. He and Don went up to Las Heras, 150 miles north of San Rafael, to see what the prospects were for renting a house large enough to start a work in and for the pastor to live in as well. They found one on the main highway in a very populated area.

At the time the dollar was high, and Don had the funds to start another work. He printed up flyers advertising the showing of the movie, *The Burning Hell,* and took the Bible institute students to pass them out door to door in that city. They showed the movie for several evenings and had preaching after the film. Many, many people came and made professions of faith. We were all very excited at the prospects of another good start to a work.

This young preacher and his very talented wife began holding services on Sundays and Wednesday nights in their front room but soon outgrew the space. The men enclosed an area in front of the house with a temporary structure made of wood and plastic. It was rather crude, but it kept out the cold and made an area big enough for the mission to grow until a building could be built. Souls were saved, and it grew.

In September 1981, the young people and men of our church approached Don about going to Las Heras to play soccer with the young men of this new work. They knew that it would be a great time of fellowship between the two works and would help the new Christians in Las Heras get to know some other Christian young people.

19

FOR THE WANT OF A NAIL, THE BATTLE WAS LOST

It was September 26, 1981, a beautiful spring day, and the young men of the church were excited and anxious to get started on the day's activities. We were traveling 150 miles north to Las Heras, Mendoza, to play a soccer game against our mission church there. The young men had been practicing for weeks, and the team was made up of twelve of our best soccer players. Six of our young people had gone by public bus early that morning. They were going as fans for their team. Our two older daughters—Judy, sixteen, and Shelley, fourteen—were part of this group. Our group actually consisted of sixteen people: my husband and me; our son, John, age twelve; our youngest daughter, Anna, age six; and the twelve players. My husband was still recuperating from a very serious gallbladder surgery and didn't have the strength to drive our truck. It did not have power steering and was very hard to drive. Since none of the young men had a driver's license, that left me to do the driving. I was not a long-distance driver, and I was really nervous about doing this.

There was another matter of concern for Don: the tires on the truck. We badly needed new tires, but we did not have the money to purchase them. Because of the economic problems in the United States, we had lost a few supporting churches, and things were really expensive in Argentina at this same time. We had just received one of those "Dear John" letters, as Don so lovingly called them, that very week. But Don knew that we were going to be making this trip. He ordered new tires by faith, praying that the funds would come in to cover the cost; however, the tires did not arrive in time. The tire dealer offered Don a new set of retreads that he assured us would work just fine for this trip. Don did not want to put those retreads on the truck, but he really didn't have a choice. So we started out.

The young men were happy, singing choruses, and having a great time. We stopped twice en route to check the tires. Everything seemed to look fine. The road condition was very poor, and Don told me not to go over fifty miles an hour. There were five of us in the front seat of the truck: Don was sitting next to me, and two young men were sitting next to him, with Anna sitting on the lap of the young man next to Don. All of a sudden there was a loud bang, and the truck starting swerving back and forth on the highway. I had never been in a situation like this before and didn't know how to react to it. I stepped on the brake, and it caused us to go sideways into the desert. The tires caught in the sand, and it literally threw the truck down a slight embankment. I remember yelling, "Oh no, here we go. Hold on tight." I'm not sure what I thought they could hold on to. We rolled over four times, and when we stopped the truck was upright on the desert floor. I only remember being thrown to the left on the first rollover. By the time the truck stopped rolling, there were cars stopping and people shouting and trying to help. They said it looked like we had hit a land mine.

Since there were no seatbelts in the truck, everyone was thrown around or out of the truck. Anna had been thrown through the front windshield. I was crushed under the steering wheel. Don and the two young men were able to get out of the truck. Don could still walk, but he couldn't move his arms. He thought he had broken his shoulders or something. He started telling others what to do and how to get me out of the truck. Since the driver's door was smashed shut, they had to actually pull me out from under the steering wheel with my arms over the top of my head. Don thought I was dead since I didn't move or respond to any of this. They laid me on the desert floor, and I briefly regained consciousness. Don said that I screamed, and it was the sweetest sound he had ever heard. All of a sudden, Don started down to the ground. His legs would no longer hold him up or work at all, but he never lost consciousness. One of the young men caught him before he hit the ground. They started to pick me up and lay me in the back of a pickup truck, and Don told them to get the bench out of the back of our truck and lay me on it. Meanwhile, they picked Don up and sat him on the front seat of the truck. They knew nothing of how to treat someone with a neck injury or possible neck injury. As soon as we were loaded into the truck bed, the man took off blowing his horn and waving a red handkerchief out the window. Don said that the man was driving about sixty miles an hour, hitting every chuckhole in the road. He hit one, and Don fell over against him. Since he could not straighten himself up, the man pushed him back up into a sitting position. Then the man hit another chuckhole, and Don fell over against the door, and he rode in that position with a broken neck for the next eight miles. He said that he felt like his body was hooked up to an electrical socket and jolt after jolt of electricity was shooting up his body. When we arrived at the first-aid station, they carried us in and put Don on a small cot. The doctor ran his hand up and down his back and said that he would be fine. He had some of our young men take Don into the men's ward and put him in a bed. They had carried me in on the truck bench, and the same doctor looked me over a little. He said, "They will both be fine. They just have some bumps and bruises from the wreck." He told them to take me into the women's ward and put me in a bed there. I had no idea how my husband really was, because I had not seen him. When they took me into the women's ward, I could hear him talking and thought he was probably OK. I was passed out most of the time, but when I would come to, I could hear him preaching. I didn't know if he had come in to check on me or not. The nurse on duty in the women's ward would not do anything for me. I was put in the bed with my street clothes on, and the pain was terrible. I asked the nurse to help me move into a more comfortable position, but she wouldn't do it. When the pain would get so bad that I could no longer stand it, I would pass out again. Meanwhile, Don was in the men's ward. They had positioned him on his side facing the wall. He had no idea how many men were in there, but he just keep preaching away. Here are his own words about the accident:

> As the driver of the pickup was driving like a maniac trying to get us to the closest medical facility, I started getting excited. I thought there was no way that I was not going to die from my injuries. I thought that any minute I was going to be face to face with my Savior. When we arrived at the first-aid station, I thought, "Now what should my last words be?" So, when one of our young men, Quiqui Garcia, opened the door, I said, "Quiqui, keep on preaching the Word." I thought, now, those were pretty good words to be remembered by. But of course, I didn't die, so I doubt that young man ever thought about it again. When they finally got me into bed, I was still very excited, but I wanted to give those men in the other beds a chance to get saved, so I started preaching to them. I said, "This is your lucky day. The Lord just let me have an accident so that I could come in here and give you the Gospel and a chance to get

saved." I couldn't see anyone, so I had no idea what they heard or what their reaction was to my declaration. But, I just kept preaching to them and telling them about Jesus.

All this time, I had no idea where they had taken Anna or John. I found out later that night that Anna been taken by ambulance to the city of Mendoza, fifty miles away. Since John had only minor injuries, he went back to San Rafael with the other young men, and was staying with the family of Dante Garcia. Judy and Shelley stayed in Mendoza to help with our care.

About nine o'clock that evening, Missionary Ray Masters came in to see us. He had flown down from the city of Cordoba, some four hundred miles away, to see how we actually were. After he landed in Mendoza, he went first to see about Anna. Then he came down to see us. After talking to Don for a few minutes, he came in to talk to me. He said, "Cherie, it isn't good. Anna has serious head injuries and a broken leg and is in a coma. They don't expect her to live through the night. Don's injuries are very serious too." I thought my heart was going to break, but I knew that somehow God would give us the grace to go through this. I still did not have a clue that Don was totally paralyzed from his neck down. No one would tell me this.

On Sunday night our dear friend, Dr. Ponce, came to see us. She was appalled that we hadn't even been seen by a doctor since entering the hospital Saturday afternoon. She drove the fifty miles to Mendoza to check on Anna and then brought a clinic doctor back to examine both of us. She told us that Anna was doing some-what better, and the hope was that she would make it, but her head injuries were very serious. The doctor checked us over the best he could under the situation. The x-ray machine was broken, so no x-rays could be taken. The doctor told me that as far as he could tell without any tests, I had some broken bones, a severe concussion, and a ruptured eardrum. They still would not tell me Don's real condition, but I could hear him talking, so I thought he was OK. I could not understand why he hadn't come in to see me.

Monday morning Don told the nurses that he wanted them to make arrangements to get us to a hospital in Mendoza. After putting a plaster cast around Don's neck, they put him on a narrow gurney and loaded him into the back of their ambulance. This ambulance was actually just an empty van with nothing but a narrow gurney in the back. Our fourteen-year-old daughter, Shelley, rode in the back with Don to keep him from falling off the gurney, holding his head all the way. The two male nurses had actually dropped him when getting him onto the gurney in the first place. You may be asking yourself by now, how in the world did he live through all of this? It was only by the merciful grace of God.

About five o'clock the ambulance returned for me. Two male nurses lifted me by the ends of the sheet to transfer me to the gurney. The sheet slipped and down I went, screaming in pain. Our daughter, Shelley, was witness to all of this, and she says that picture has always remained in her mind. When we arrived in Mendoza, they wheeled me into the maternity ward so Don and I could be in the same room. It was the only available room with two beds in it. When they wheeled me in, Don said, "Well, honey, looks like we are going to get that second honeymoon that we always wanted."

I still had not seen Don since the accident, and if I hadn't heard those words from him, I don't think I would have believed it was really Don. His head was as large as a basketball and black and blue. His face hung over the plaster neck cast. I could hardly believe that this was my husband. Soon after I arrived, they took him to x-ray his neck and put him in a larger cast. He told me later that he had never suffered pain like the pain that shot through his body when they put that cast on him. They brought him back to the room, and the nurses worked and worked with a hand crank trying to get the bed in a comfortable position for him. His pain was excruciating. The nurses were so kind and gentle with both of us, but they were angry and humiliated about the treatment we had received at the first-aid station. When we arrived at the hospital in Mendoza, we still had on the clothes that we were wearing at the time of the accident. I had rocks and sand and broken glass in the back of my sweater. The nurses cleaned us up and did everything possible to make us comfortable.

The next morning the doctor who put the cast on Don came in with a neurosurgeon. They had a small ball of yarn and tried to place it in Don's right hand. It just rolled off onto the floor. I asked them why he couldn't close his hand around the yarn, and that is when I realized for the first time that he was totally paralyzed from his neck down. The shock of that moment was horrible, and I realized just how close I had come to losing my husband. I cried and prayed that God would heal him, but the prognosis was that he would never leave his bed again. For the next three weeks, Ray Masters stayed by our bedside helping to take care of us. His wife, Virginia, flew down to help with our care and with Anna's care. People from our mission church came to help as much as possible. Anna was in another hospital but under the care of a neurosurgeon who had studied in Oklahoma City. He was actually the best neurosurgeon in Mendoza at the time. God was watching over our little girl. Our two daughters, Judy and Shelley, would go between the two hospitals to help with our care, and Judy handled the money end of the situation. All the medical and hospital bills had to be paid in dollars at the time of service. She would have to go between the hospital and the pharmacy to buy all of the medicines and medical supplies we needed, such as bandages, tape, and wound-cleansing lotions. The hospital was not equipped with the medicines and other supplies. She would have to go to the exchange house each day to get the money for medicines and the doctors. She was sixteen years old and handled all of this responsibility.

She'd go to San Rafael on the weekends and play the organ for the services, teach her Sunday school class, pay the bills, do the laundry, and bring back whatever we needed for our care.

Shelley had the biggest part of the responsibility of taking care of Anna. She was fourteen. Our oldest daughter, Donna, came after a few weeks to help with everything. And of course, our son, John, was staying with Dante Garcia's family in San Rafael. This accident took its toll on all of the kids. For many years some of them could not talk about it at all. It just stayed so fresh in their minds that they could not handle reliving it. Lifetime scars were left on everyone involved in this horrendous mishap.

After three and a half weeks, Anna and I were released from the hospitals. A young man in the church in Las Heras had an unfinished house that he let us use until Don was out of the hospital. The church provided us with some beds and a table, and we brought in the benches from our truck, which was totaled. This became our home for the next two months. Don spent another four weeks in the hospital, and he began to regain some movement in his arms and legs. He was now classified as an "incomplete quad." The doctors were amazed at this development. After two months of being hospitalized, the doctors knew that there was actually nothing else they could do for Don, so they discharged him. We asked what he could do for physical therapy. The doctor said, "Well, you need to walk a lot and squeeze a ball." Don could not stand and could barely bend his arms. His hands would close, but he could not reopen them.

Up until this time, we hadn't planned on returning to the United States. But we now knew the only way Don was going to get better was to return to the States and get some real physical therapy. We had to wait another three weeks until Don was strong enough so we could at least drag him up the steps of the small plane to Chile. It took three of us to do it. Praise God that this flight was only thirty minutes long. He was in a body cast from his head down past his waist. I was in a body cast from under my arms down to my hips, and Anna was in a cast from her hip down. We were quite a sight. When we arrived in Chile, the airline gave us three seats a piece so we could lie down most of the way. God was so merciful to us.

Brother Joe Hensley, one of Don's early converts in Long Beach, met us at the airport to transport us to Long Beach Memorial Hospital. God put us all in the hands of a wonderful surgeon there. They took us in for x-ray and CAT scans. When they were wheeling Don down the hall, there were technicians running along behind him, asking him where in the world he had been to have a cast like the one he had. They said that they had not seen anything like it for more than thirty years. That just about summed up the medical situation in Argentina at that time. But, praise God, we were all still alive, and the doctors had done the best they could for us there. When Don was x-rayed, they were surprised to see that his seventh vertebra was literally hanging off the sixth vertebra, pinching the spinal cord. This was not even in the x-rays from Argentina. The surgeon said, "Don, we have to put you right in the hospital and get you into traction." They told us that if they had removed the cast in Argentina (which they had planned on doing in a month or so), that the smallest bump or fall would have severed his spinal cord, and he would have died. They were amazed that he hadn't already died from all of it.

They drilled holes in the sides of his head and bolted a strip of metal over the top. They put him in a striker frame and hooked a sandbag onto the metal strip. They would turn this striker frame over once an hour. He would hang by his face for an hour at a time and then back on his backside for an hour. This went on for twelve days, but the results were not what they had hoped they would be. After twelve days they put him into a "halo." It was bolted into in his skull with four bolts. He felt every bit of this procedure. The pain was excruciating for him, plus there was the pressure of them drilling the holes. Then they took him into surgery and took a piece of bone from his hip and fused it into his neck at the sixth and seventh vertebrae. The doctor had told us that this would leave him totally paralyzed, but at least he would live. When he came out of the surgery, the doctor was shaking his head. His first words to us were, "I don't believe what is happening in there. He is already moving his toes. This just isn't possible." He didn't know the Great Physician and His healing powers.

After a few days they began physical therapy. Don was in the hospital for several weeks, and by the time he was discharged, he was walking with our help. We were staying in an apartment right there at the hospital. Every day we would take him for physical therapy, and every day he would make a little more progress. Something began to really bother him. At the time, there were two young men in rehab with him with the same injury, but they were both completely paralyzed from their necks down. They watched him every day making progress, and they were basically staying exactly the same. He witnessed to both of them, and they listened, but they were very angry young men. It began to wear on Don to see the pain in their eyes as they watched him improve daily. He finally asked the doctor to reassign him to another physical therapy department, which they did.

In February, we received a phone call from Don's former pastor, Don Stone. He was now pastoring in Hawaii. He flew to California to visit us. After he returned to Hawaii, he called us again. This time he had wonderful news for us. His church wanted to fly us all to Oahu to live as long as Don needed to recuperate. They gave us a home to live in, a car to drive, and enrolled our children in their Christian school. What a tremendous blessing and help that was.

We lived there for six wonderful months. During that time Don remained in physical therapy and grew stronger every day. He was still in his halo and had to sleep sitting up in a chair, but he was comfortable and rested wonderfully. One night, though, he was sound asleep, and a gecko dropped from the ceiling and landed on his head. It scared him and he jumped, hitting a wall and causing a picture to fall off the wall and hit him on top of his head. He said that it really rang his bell, and his whole body vibrated from the impact of the picture frame hitting the metal halo. Praise God there was not any permanent damage done. (This is another one of those stories that should have been entered in "Espinosa's Believe it or Not.")

After five months Don and I flew back to California to get the halo removed. He asked the doctor if he could start playing golf. The doctor laughed and said, "Don, just a few months ago, you were in the grips of death, and now you want to go out and play golf! Go for it!" Don was excited but received a real shock the first day out. He had no idea how weak he really was at this point. He swung at the ball, and it literally just rolled off the tee and stopped. I had not seen him discouraged until that moment. He could hardly believe he was that weak. But it didn't stop him. Each day I would take him out to the course, and he would try again. He progressed to the point where he could hit it a hundred or so yards. Every day he'd work hard at therapy to get stronger. He was now very excited and anxious to get back to the field to continue to work for the Lord. By the end of the year, we were on our way back to Argentina. He had fully recovered his strength and was ready to do a greater work for the Lord.

In later years Don would use the illustration of the poem "For the Want of a Nail" to tell about how important it was for the churches to continue to support their missionaries on the field.

For the Want of a Nail

For want of a nail the shoe was lost.
For want of a shoe the horse was lost.
For want of a horse the rider was lost.
For want of a rider the battle was lost.
For want of a battle the kingdom was lost.
And all for the want of a horseshoe nail.

He used this illustration to show that because one person might have stopped giving to missions, a missionary was nearly taken off the field, and that could have caused the battle for souls on that field to be lost.

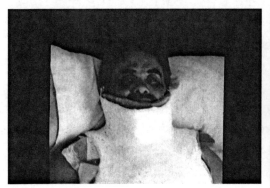

Three weeks after the accident

Eight months after accident

20

HEADING HOME AT LAST

WE LEFT BEAUTIFUL Hawaii with its soft breezes at the end of July and moved to Springfield, Missouri. My sweet, wonderful husband was willing to go through the hottest part of the summer months with the sweltering Midwestern heat and humidity, because I wanted to help my family. They were going through some very hard trials.

After spending a couple of months in Springfield, Missouri, we headed to California to pack up our crates. Roy and Cleta Hendrickson were the founders and hard workers of Fellowship Crating at the time. We had been buying some things to take back to the field, and we were going there to finish crating up everything. On our trip from Missouri to California, our family was in high spirits. We were all excited about heading home at last. We were going to be on a plane in just three days to go home. After spending a few minutes talking to Roy and Cleta, I went into the warehouse to wash my hands in the bathroom.

When I came out, I felt as if someone had come behind me and stuck a knife in my back. My legs went out from under me, and I fell to the floor. I could not get up, so I called for Don to come help me. He and Roy put me into our car and drove to the nearest hospital. They examined me, took x-rays, and said that I had a ruptured disk in my lower back, and it was going to be three or four months after surgery before we would be able to go back to Argentina. Until that moment, we had no doubt whatsoever that God wanted us back on the field. Our kids began to cry because of the disappointment. For the first time since our accident, we wondered if God was trying to tell us He didn't want us to return. How could that be when He had performed such a miracle in Don's life?

Don called the surgeon who had operated on him in Long Beach, and the doctor said to bring me right to Memorial Hospital. He made arrangements for me to be hospitalized there. He ran some tests, and sure enough the disk was ruptured, but it was just a hairline rupture. He told us that he was not even going to put me on pain medicine yet, because he wanted to see if the pain would be less as each day went by. Meanwhile I had to lie on my back in bed without turning over or trying to get up. Praise God, each day I began to feel a bit less pain. I was hospitalized for ten days. We were anxious to try to return to Argentina as quickly as possible, but the doctor said the only way he would permit me to go was if I attended a six-week "back school" and learned how to do everything without damaging my back more. Six weeks seemed like a lifetime, but we had to do it. God again provided an apartment there in the hospital, and we set up housekeeping for six or seven weeks. I had literally lost at least 50 percent of my strength and had to work hard to regain it.

After a period of ten weeks, we were heading home at last. At the time we had no idea why God had allowed this to happen, but talking about it later, we began to realize what a disaster it would have been if my back had gone out just as soon as we returned home. God, by His wonderful grace, had helped us through another trial and taught us to trust Him more than ever.

21

GOD'S BLESSINGS ON THE WORK

A FEW WEEKS before we left Hawaii, we received news that our storage room had been broken into. Many things had been stolen. It was a real heartbreak when we found out that some of the same young men who had been in the accident with us were the ones who did this. They were tried and put in prison. Many of their relatives were members of our church, and we really didn't know what kind of reception we would have upon returning. Thankfully, they received us back with open arms. We were so happy to be back, even though we had to return to our adobe house, which was already beginning to crumble around us. We had to make some changes in our home and fix what we were working on at the time of the accident, but it was so great to be back with our people. Don felt as if God had given him a precious gift to be able to continue working with the people he loved so much. He was so grateful for this opportunity to continue serving the Lord. He wanted to get as much done as he could in the time he had left.

We returned to our home in San Rafael in December 1982. In our absence Dante Garcia had pastored the church. That was quite a feat for an eighteen-year-old kid, but the attendance went down very little that year. On the eighth of August, 1982, the church celebrated "Children's Day," and they had 315 in attendance with thirty-eight saved. He did a tremendous job, and God blessed him with 232 souls saved that year. Winning souls to Christ has always been one of Dante's first priorities, and as the scripture says in Proverbs 11:30, "...he that winneth souls is wise." God truly gave this young man wisdom beyond his years.

The peso had devaluated while we were recuperating in the States. Upon returning we were able to rent a building downtown and set it up as offices for the church and for Don. We also had a reception area, where two of our daughters, Judy, then seventeen, and Shelley, now fifteen, worked during the day giving out correspondence courses, correcting them, and giving out the new books. This turned out to be a very fruitful ministry, and it was wonderful to see our daughters involved in it. This was not a paying job, but it was a great ministry for them. We were in this building for several months.

Meanwhile we were building a new addition to our house, which was badly needed. It was a two-story building that we connected to the old adobe house. The addition included an office for Don, a huge office for the church staff, a combination workout room to continue his physical therapy, and a large space to host work groups preparing for vacation bible schools, "Good News" clubs, and Sunday school materials. After being cramped into a small area doing all of the above, we were thrilled to have all of this new space. During the year we were recuperating from our injuries, God not only supplied all of our needs but also gave us extra funds so we could build this building.

Shortly after we returned home, Don asked Luis Yañez to work full time for the church. We now had two full-time workers, and Don began to train him just as he had Dante. He took Luis with him everywhere he went to teach him how to take care of church business and deal with the authorities in getting building permits and permits for different activities. He also taught him how to deal with the lawyers and notaries in securing business papers, etc. Luis was already teaching the young people's class in Sunday school and was really busy with activities for the class. He had also been using his trade as a builder to erect a small building behind the church to use as a nursery and classroom. Many times Luis came into the office and asked Don if he could build something that would give us more space in our rented building. This was all done on his own time before he came on staff. He was a hard worker, and Don saw a lot of potential in him.

I wish I could say that all went well from that moment on, but that's not even reality. As Don's staff grew, so did the potential problems, and Satan always knows where to attack, but praise God, Dante and Luis got along wonderfully and worked together as a team. Don was able to delegate more of the practical work and also the time-consuming business negotiations of getting permits from the government, standing in lines at the bank to pay bills, and doing the business end of the work. With more staff members, we were also able to begin more Good News clubs and other ministries. All of this left Don free to deal more on the spiritual end of the ministry. God really began to bless the work, and it began to grow very quickly.

22

TO GOD BE THE GLORY

I Cor. 1:31: "He that glorieth let him glory in the Lord."

WE WERE EXCITED about what God was doing, and the people had such a heart to work and serve the Lord. We had many preaching conferences with special speakers, big Sundays, and special days. The exchange went back and forth so much that we never knew one day to the next what the dollar would be worth. When it was high, we took advantage of it and invested it all in new ministries.

We started the year 1983 with 106 in attendance the first Sunday. We started showing the film *The Burning Hell* in more neighborhood plazas and also continued showing it and other films each weekend at the church. On the weekend of January 21, over seven hundred people came out to watch these films, and we had seventy professions of faith made. Did they all get gloriously saved? We would like to think so, but that would not be realistic, but praise God many of them did and began to come to church, were baptized, and grew in knowledge and faith.

We also started a monthly ministry in a mountain village called El Sosneado. We started out with a film and were able to generate a lot of interest in the people in hearing the Word of God preached. The town council loaned us a building that had housed a restaurant in past years. It was now used only on special occasions. We would take some of the Bible institute students each month to help us pass out tracts and invite people to come to the services. This was another fruitful ministry.

In December we had our first Faith Promise Mission Conference. We took on six national missionaries, and missions became an intricate part of our church. The people were very enthusiastic about this new ministry. As they began to give to missions, we began to see them not only grow in grace, but God began to bless them financially. Our Bible institute was full of young people excited to learn more of God's Word and how to win souls. We trained these young people to teach children and how to win them to Christ. We never had a need for workers, because they all wanted to be part of everything we did. Many of the adults would take their vacation time during Vacation Bible School so they could work in it. We still see that happening today.

By the end of 1983, there were 943 professions of faith and an attendance of 303. Our high day that year was 557 on Children's Day.

The following year, 1984, we had a planning meeting where we laid out a year's calendar. Don added more special days and Sunday school campaigns. The month of September had a special day every Sunday of the month. It's been twenty-nine years since Don initiated September as a month of four special Sundays, and all four of the works still follow that plan.

On February 14, 1984, Don had the first of several grand mal epileptic seizures. It lasted several minutes and did a lot of damage to his brain cells. They did a brain wave test, CT scan, and x-rays of his head. The tests showed the deterioration of many brain cells, but the doctors thought that he would be fine after a few days. They could not determine what had caused the seizure but said he would probably be on meds for the rest of his life, and he was. He literally lost four days of his life. He was hospitalized for four days and couldn't remember any part of what happened during this time. It took him a couple of weeks to regain his strength. The possibility of more seizures didn't stop him from carrying on the work. It seemed as if Satan was determined to stop the work of the Lord from going forth, but praise God it didn't.

We started fifteen new Good News clubs in neighborhoods all over San Rafael, some as far as ten miles out in the country. The combined attendance was way over five hundred children. We then ran our buses into these neighborhoods to pick the kids up on Sunday morning, but this bus ministry was special, because it brought in whole families. The dollar was high, and we started renting four or five buses besides the two we owned. Don knew that we were maxed out as far as room went. We had the two army tents out in back of the church for classrooms and tried heating them with kerosene heaters. It didn't do much good when it snowed, and the temperatures were below freezing. In the summertime they roasted in the tents, but we were doing the best we could do at the time. One Sunday one of the children came running into the auditorium, yelling that the tent had fallen down. It had snowed so hard that the tents, literally, had sunk in from the weight of the snow and caused the heavy wooden poles to collapse. No one was hurt, but we knew we had to obtain better and bigger facilities.

Don began to pray and look for a piece of property that we could buy to build our own facilities. He was very aware of the location, because he knew how important this was. Our city was growing to the south of San Rafael. He talked to architects to get their input on the best location. The following is part of a newsletter that Don wrote in March 1984.

Once again with the help of faithful Pastors and Churches, God has given me the desire of my heart to Glorify Him here in Argentina. (Psalms 37:4). When you received my last newsletter with the pictorial report of what has been happening in the work, I told you of the immense undertaking of faith we were about to embark upon, the procurement of a beautiful piece of property. It is located in the ideal location in all of the city of San Rafael to build a Church and Sunday school. Praise the Lord, we now have the land. The great missionary, William Cary, said, "Attempt great things for God and expect great things from God." This is what we are attempting to do here in San Rafael.

The piece of property had been owned by a man who had hung on to it for over thirty years with no desire to sell it. It had been in this man's family since the founding of San Rafael. When Don approached him about buying it, the man laughed and said, "You know, I was just thinking the other day that it is about time to get this land off my hands." God had already been working on him. Don used to say when God created the earth, He looked down and saw that land in San Rafael and said, "That piece of land is going to be used for the Templo Bautista de San Rafael (San Rafael Baptist Temple)."

Some may criticize others when numbers become an important factor in their ministry. Don was all about numbers—not to build the biggest church in Argentina, or to glorify himself, but because each one was a soul that needed the Gospel. The following are some excerpts from Don's newsletters to our supporting pastors telling of the blessings throughout the year of 1984:

742-667

Numbers, Numbers, Numbers! Would you believe that after nearly three years of waiting, I finally have a telephone in my house? But 745-667 is not my phone number. They are far more important than that. They are numbers that signify the blessing of God in the work here in San Rafael, Mendoza, Argentina. Seven hundred forty-two indicates our

Sunday morning attendance a few weeks ago with ninety-one saved in that service. Why are these numbers important? My point of view has always been: Thank God for seven people in Sunday school (we have had that, my family and one other), but twenty is better. Thank God for twenty, but fifty is better. Thank God for fifty, but one hundred is better. Thank God for one hundred, but two hundred is better. Thank God for two hundred, but five hundred is better. Thank God for five hundred, but seven hundred forty-two is better. Thank God for seven hundred forty-two, but…is better. Better because each number represents a precious soul that Christ died for and that He wants to hear His precious Gospel.

Six hundred sixty-seven indicates the number of precious Argentines who have made a profession of faith in the work here in San Rafael through the first five months of this year, an average of over thirty per week. The criticism goes like this: "How do you know they really got saved?" I don't, but one thing I do know is they at least had the chance to. They heard the Word, responded to it by coming forward after hearing, had the Gospel further explained to them, and then with their mouths called on the Lord Jesus Christ to enter their hearts and be their Savior. That's how you and I got saved. The rest is between them and God.

POOR DEVIL LOSES 70 DISCIPLES

Greetings from the Harvest field. I hope you all are enjoying the blessings of the Lord as we are in the work here in Argentina.

"Poor Devil Loses Seventy Disciples"—let me explain: Our winter (your summer) has ended and spring (your fall) has come, so we have begun our outdoor meetings once again. What we do is go into the neighborhood plazas all over our city and surrounding cities every Friday and Saturday night with a Gospel team from the church and show the film The Burning Hell. *In Latin America, each barrio (neighborhood) has a name. We started this year in a barrio named Pobre Diablo,*

which means "Poor Devil." We had a great turnout, and seventy people made professions of faith in Christ. And Praise the Lord! Thirty-four of those people were in church Sunday morning. Please pray for me that I will have the physical and spiritual strength to do all that is in my heart to do.

WHAT A YEAR!
December 1984

I praise God for the strength He has given me to be able to be here in Argentina. Three years ago today (Dec. 3, 1981), I was operated on for my broken neck. The doctors thought I would be paralyzed for life, but God truly worked a miracle, and by His Grace here I am. Tomorrow, Dec. 4, I will be fifty years young (unbelievable, no?). I'm looking forward to many more fruitful years in the Lord's service. I just want to keep on winning souls till He comes. Pray for me. This was the greatest year thus far in my twenty-two years of preaching the glorious Gospel of Christ.

23

REACHING THE REGIONS BEYOND

WE WERE EXCITED about the prospects of what was before us. The church family was growing and eager to work and win more souls to Christ. God kept laying new ministries on Don's heart and the funds to begin them. In his January newsletter, he wrote:

ANOTHER OPEN DOOR

Yes! God has opened another door for us to reach a greater number of souls for Him and His kingdom. Let me share what is happening: It has been on my heart for years to reach the shepherds and gauchos in the Andes Mountains with the Gospel. We have done so with limited success. About a year and a half ago, we started a work in the small mountain village of El Sosneado, a village of about 250 people.

In January, nine of us from the church here in San Rafael went to El Sosneado to have a Vacation Bible School. VBS was held in the daytime and Evangelistic services each night. I drove my pickup truck 20 miles up into the mountains to bring the children each morning. I took them home after VBS and made the return trip in the evening with the adults and teenagers. After the service I would take them back home. This meant 160 miles a day, 800 miles for the week, on terrible mountain roads in the Andes. I got stuck in the mud three times, but praise the Lord, it was worth it. For the week, there were 44 adults and teenagers saved and 40 children received Christ in the VBS. The last night there were over 100 in the service and 30 of them came in the back of my pickup (now that's loaded!). But with all of this, we did so little of what is really needed to do. Beyond the 20 miles that I was able to get to, there are many other families that also need the Gospel. On the other side of the river from where I picked up the people are various other families. Through the years we have distributed 250 sets of Gospel records with cardboard players to hear the Gospel messages. But still our hearts are burdened for the others scattered over the Andes here in southern Mendoza who are without the Gospel. NOW God has opened the door to reach ALL of them by means of radio. I found out that Radio Malargue has a special type of transmission that reaches into the canyons and valleys in the mountains, as well as the city of Malargue, a city of 20,000 people. On the 18th of February we began to broadcast the Gospel for one half hour at 5:00 p.m. Monday through Friday. On the 1st of March we had our monthly service in El Sosneado, and there were 54 in the service. Everyone there was listening every day to the broadcast. So praise God. Not only are we reaching the lost, but at the same time we are feeding the sheep!

Our convert and young preacher, Dante Garcia, was doing all of the preaching and teaching on this broadcast. That young man has been instrumental in thousands coming to know Christ as their Savior. During the many years that Dante preached this broadcast, he learned his Bible from cover to cover.

Through the years we have seen countless shepherds and their families come to the Lord as a result of this ministry. Dante started a mission church in Malargue, and he has seen many of those who were saved in the mountain regions move into town and become faithful followers of Christ. Times are changing, and many of the children of the shepherds have left the mountains and moved into large cities. We are praying that the messages they heard while growing up will bring forth much fruit in the future.

24

WHILE THE MEN BUILT THE BUILDING, THE BUILDING BUILT THE MEN

On March 31st we laid the cornerstone for our new building in San Rafael! It was a time of great rejoicing for our people and much publicized even in our city. The press and television covered the story, showing pictures of our services, the projected building, and me laying the

cornerstone. There is much interest in what "those Baptists are doing."
The Lord is continuing to bless. We have seen 300 souls come to Christ
in the last three months. On Easter we had 547 in Sunday school; two
weeks before there were 625; and Holy Week there were 52 saved in spe-
cial services, 48 adults and young people. The people are reachable, but
we must have room to put them.

As YOU CAN tell from this newsletter excerpt, Don was excited about
what was happening. It seemed that God was blessing every new
endeavor with more souls. Everyone was excited seeing the church
was growing by leaps and bounds, and everyone wanted to be a
part of building this new church. Many bought bags of cement,
and some bought bricks. But the amazing thing was the way the
men of the church worked to build this building. Don had hired a
construction company to build the building, but after a few weeks
he began to see many flaws in the construction. Measurements
were off enough that the foundation not laid out straight. He fired
this company, and Luis Yañez became the head of construction.
Although he hired a few outside workers, including some of the
men of the church who were out of a job, most of the work was
done voluntarily by the men of the church. They were not paid for
this work but gave of their time and effort to build the house of
God. Some worked every day their off hours. Others gave up their
weekends and holidays to work. The following is from Don's newsletter dated August 1985:

The best news is the way the new church building is going up so quickly
here in San Rafael. By faith we have expanded the Sunday school to
take care of another 300 people, making a total capacity of over a thou-
sand. The added room will not be a great expense, because the men
of the church are doing most of the work. I now know how Nehemiah
must have felt when he and the other Jews accomplished so much in so
little time as they built the walls of Jerusalem. Neh. 4:6: "So we built
the wall…for the people had a mind to work." What a blessing it is for

me to see the way the men of the church love the Lord and are willing to sacrifice their time to work. The last two national holidays, June 20th, Flag Day, and July 9th, Independence Day, there were 26 and 27 men respectively working on the building. Needless to say we accomplished a great deal. I hope to have this building completed inside and out by November 3rd, which is the eighth anniversary of the church.

Many of these men had been hit and miss in their church attendance until they started volunteering to help with the construction. As they worked together with the faithful men of the church, they started becoming more faithful in their attendance and consequently began to grow in grace and knowledge of our Lord Jesus Christ. What a blessing it was to see these men working together. The community began to take notice, and some were saying that Pastor Espinosa was making slaves out of the members of the church. Others asked how he got them to work so hard, especially on the holidays. Don explained they were doing this because it was their church, and their love for the souls in San Rafael was encouraging them to get this building up in the shortest time possible. The ladies of the church would fix lunch for them, and in the evenings Don would have an "asado" for them. An *asado* is an Argentine barbeque. Everyone was involved in one way or another. It was a great and exciting time.

But of course Satan is never happy when the work of God is going strong. He began to put obstacles in the way of finishing the building by November. There were, of course, jobs that had to be contracted out, such as the metal beams and steel roof. They kept promising that the job would be done by a certain time, and then there were delays. People outside the church weren't as anxious as we were to finish the house of God.

Once a year in the month of October, the Fundamental Baptist Congress was sponsored and held in one of the churches. Two years before, Don had offered to host it in San Rafael. We were extremely busy getting everything ready for this conference during the construction of the church. It was a huge undertaking. There would be up to three hundred guests coming in from all over Argentina, Uruguay, Chile, and Paraguay. Most of the missionaries would stay in hotels, but the national pastors and lay people were usually accommodated by the host church. This meant that we would need space to sleep around two hundred guests. Also, we had to have a place to prepare and serve the meals. When Don had offered to host the meeting, we hoped to have our building finished enough that the visitors could sleep and eat there. The roofing man kept promising that it would be done in time, but there was one holdup after another. He kept saying, "No hay problema, pastor." When you translate this, it means, "No problem, Pastor." But it was turning out to be a huge problem.

It was one week before the conference, and we still did not have a roof. We had already planned to hold the services in our old building, but there was no way that two hundred people could sleep and eat there. Don wanted to make it as inexpensive as possible for the visitors so that many could come. Three days before the conference, the roofing company had put up the beams but still had not put on the steel panels, each one having to be connected with dozens of bolts. Meanwhile Don was working on plan B. We had contacted all the hotels in town to get the best prices and even looked into renting a restaurant if it came to that. It would have cost us a fortune to do it this way, but Don was willing to do it to be able to host this meeting. He had planned to have seminars on each ministry that we were doing in our church. His heart's desire was to help these national pastors learn more ways of reaching souls for Christ.

By God's wonderful grace, the roofing company worked all night to finish putting on the roof. The owner proudly said to Don, "See, Pastor Espinosa, I told you there was no problem." It probably was another reason for adding gray to Don's hair. God doesn't always do things according to our plans, but He does do it according to His. We had a great meeting, and the visitors were thrilled to death with the accommodations and the food. The women of the church worked so hard cooking and cleaning that week. The building wasn't done, but it was done enough that we could use it that week.

When Don drew up the plans for the church, he designed it in a way that we could host big meetings. He built large shower rooms, extra bathrooms, and large classrooms. We put in a large kitchen and work area. God gave him a love for souls and a vision to teach others how to reach them. Over and over he showed the truth of his life scriptures, **I Corinthians 9:19 and 22b: "...I made myself servant unto all, that I might gain the more...I am made all things to all men, that I might by all means save some."**

25

BIGGER AND GREATER THINGS AHEAD

1037 Is Great—2,500 Is Greater
March 1986

We are truly enjoying the blessings of God here in Argentina in 1986 as never before. Our record Sunday school attendance had been 742, and that in a rented stadium, but on January 5th we had 1,037 in Sunday school with 80 saved in the old church building. Then on February

1st we had 2,500 in a special service in a rented auditorium with 96 saved.

As you can see, we really need our new church building that we have been building for the last eleven months, and Lord willing we will be moving into it in three weeks. God has been good to us as our supporting churches have given to make this possible. The people in the church have given over $5,000 US dollars and have worked thousands of hours without pay to build a beautiful church building that will take care of over 1,000 people, and by the grace of God we are going to fill it up for His Glory.

WE ARE IN!!!
June 1986

By the grace of God and the sacrifices of God's people, both in Argentina and in the United States, we have moved into our new building in San Rafael, Mendoza, Argentina. **What a miracle of God!** *We moved in just eleven and one half months after we laid the cornerstone on March 31, 1985. The people of San Rafael have never seen a building go up so fast. So we now have a building that will comfortably take care of over 1,000 souls. With God's help, and the tremendous spirit to work and win souls among the Argentines, we will someday see this building overflowing like the other building.* *"HE IS ABLE."*

THESE TWO NEWSLETTERS tell in just a few words how involved the people of the church were in the building of our new facilities. This was their church, and they were proud to have had a part in it. Most of the funds came from the sacrificial giving of God's people in our supporting churches, but the members of Templo Bautista de San Rafael had not only sacrificed their time and talents but sacrificed also of their very limited funds. The church family consisted mostly of the poorer-class people, but as God's Word says in **Matthew 6:21, "For where your treasure is, there will your heart be also."** During the construction of God's house, the people grew in grace and knowledge of the Word of God. They became more faithful in their service to our Lord and serious about filling up the house of God with more souls.

⟨∞⟩

In July 1986 Don received a letter from the Baptist Bible Tribune asking him to write about his ministry and his work as a missionary of the Baptist Bible Fellowship. The following is the article that he wrote:

TO WIN A LARGER NUMBER

By Missionary Don Espinosa—San Rafael, Mendoza, Argentina

The Scripture verse that I have chosen for my life's work on the mission field is I Corinthians 9:19: "...I have made myself servant unto all, that I might gain the more." I like the last part of that verse even better in the Spanish text, which reads "para ganar a mayor número." It translates "to win a larger number." This is exactly what we are trying to do.

When at Baptist Bible College I had the privilege of sitting at the feet of Dr. Fred S. Donnelson. His mission philosophy was "Reproduce on the mission field what the great churches in the States were doing." While pastoring for six years in California before coming to Argentina, I had the opportunity of fellowshipping with some great pastors who taught me many things about building a church for the Lord. I also had some great evangelists come and hold revivals, such Joe Boyd, Jack Garner and Jim Lyons. Each one of these spiritual men taught me something on how to "win a larger number." I attended Dr. Jack Hyles's Pastor School. This was a tremendous blessing and taught me a great lesson about how to win a larger number to Christ.

When we arrived here in San Rafael nine years ago, I was determined to use everything I'd learned at Baptist Bible College and from these great and wise men. I was also determined to go through every door that the Lord would open for me to win a larger number for Him and for His Kingdom. I had decided that the way to attack Satan's dominion was with a "Saturation Ministry." The more seed sown, the larger the harvest would be.

The following are some of the ministries that we currently have:

1. A solid church here in San Rafael
2. A Bible Institute
3. A mission church
4. Eleven Good News Bible Clubs
5. An open-air film ministry in the Spring and Fall
6. A daily radio broadcast reaching a 300-mile area of the evangelized souls in the Andes Mountains. This also reaches into Chile.
7. Correspondence courses
8. Weekly television ads
9. A strong visitation program.
10. Distribution of the "Sword of the Lord" and trying to reach approximately 100 English-speaking people in our area.
11. Putting the finishing touches on our new church building

Five years ago we had a near-fatal accident on the field. My neck was broken and I was paralyzed for three months. My wife and youngest daughter suffered severe injuries and were nearly killed. But the Lord raised us up and allowed us to come back to Argentina to our field of service.

To His Glory, there have been over 5,000 professions of faith in Christ in the three and one half years since we returned. Pray that God will continue to open new doors for us and that we will have the strength and wisdom to go through them.

Happy in the work? Definitely! Satisfied? No! We want to, by the Grace of God, "win an even larger number to Him."

The blessings that year were tremendous, but Satan was also busy working. Don began to wear out physically. We thought at first it was just the after effects of the building program. But it seemed that every day he would go full speed until about 10:00 in the morning, and he would "hit the wall" so to speak. In San Rafael we still had the siesta time when everything was closed from noon until four in the afternoon. This was very frustrating to Don, because he had so much he had to do during this building program, and most of it had to be done before noon. But he just had to stop about 10:00 a.m. He was so tired that he couldn't go on. For the first time, I began to see changes in Don that were normally foreign to his personality. He had always been an up guy, seeing the positive side of things. Things began to bother him that had never been important before. He was frustrated, and so was I. During this time he had to return to the States for a few weeks to preach a mission conference. One morning he was getting dressed. He sneezed, and an electrical shock ran down his left arm. He said it was like he had just stuck his finger in light socket. That sneeze had caused a pinched nerve coming from his injured spinal column. He was in excruciating pain. He couldn't stand to have the slightest breeze on his arm. He had to always wear long-sleeved shirts and kept his hand covered. If someone patted him on the back, the pain was so severe that he would actually be out of commission for two or three days at a time. There was so much he wanted to do, and he didn't have the strength to do much of it. The doctors there in San Rafael didn't seem to have a clue what was the matter with him. He needed some answers and some help.

26

WHEN I AM WEAK, THEN AM I STRONG

WE HAD PLANNED to take a year's furlough in 1987. Don had already written to his supporting churches to schedule them, but he began to wonder how in the world he would be able to keep these commitments with the physical problems he was having. One thing he did know was that God had never failed him yet.

If you were a resident in Argentina in 1987, you could buy a "visit USA" ticket for under $400. You could fly into twelve or fourteen different cities of your choice for that price. Don set up his furlough to be gone for two weeks at a time and then home for two weeks to report to the churches that were close by. Because of the pain in his back and arm, he couldn't drive long distances. It would literally exhaust him to the point that he could barely function. But he also wanted to use God's money wisely and make it go as far as possible. He was very conscious of every penny that God gave us to do His work. With the visit USA ticket, he would sometimes fly to out-of-the-way places to build up his air miles. By doing this he had enough air miles saved up to purchase four return tickets to Argentina without costing a cent.

Don left the church under the leadership of our national pastor, Dante Garcia. He was now twenty-two years old and had already been preaching on the radio every day for over two years. We knew that God had His hand on this young man and was going to use him in a marvelous way.

Our first thing to take care of when we arrived in the states, was to go to our daughter, Shelley's, graduation from college in Springfield, Missouri. We left immediately after the graduation ceremony and went to Kansas to marry her off to a young Kansas man that she met while attending Bible College. It was a very busy two weeks, but we had a wonderful time. It actually went very well. Not one single mishap. We felt like it was going to be a very good year.

JULY 1987

We are now on furlough and will be here in the States for about a year. The works have been left entirely in the hands of the national pastors and workers. Please pray for them as it is their first time to be completely "solo." I received a great report today from Pastor Garcia in San Rafael. There were sixty saved in the last month, so that's great news.

SEPTEMBER 1987

News from the field: The Lord is continuing to bless. Last month they had a big day of 653 in Sunday school with 119 professions of faith in Christ on that day alone. There have been a few problems in the church, but God has given the national pastors the wisdom to solve them.
News about my health: I had a small operation since my last newsletter. They did a "nerve block" on my neck. It was supposed to take care of 90% of the pain I am having from a pinched nerve in my neck...
It didn't work, and doctors are saying that I will probably need neck

surgery again. They also found out that I have diabetes, which they are treating with medicine, diet, and exercise.

DECEMBER 1987

Thank you for your prayers for my health. The pinched nerve in my neck is painful, but I can live with it. I was advised by the surgeon who operated on my neck after I broke it in the accident to not have another neck surgery which could leave me with worse pain and possible paralysis. He said if I could stand the pain it would be better to just live with it. So continue to pray for me that God will give me the physical strength to continue working for Him.

I recently spoke to Pastor Dante Garcia in San Rafael, and he said there has been someone saved in every service since we left. He said that an evangelist preached last Wednesday night, and there were thirty-eight saved. I know you will rejoice with me for a great report like that.

FEBRUARY 1988

In December I went to Argentina for two weeks to see how the works were getting along. Since it was the first time for the nationals to be on their own, I told them before I left that I would try to come down in the middle of our furlough. What a blessing it was to see the people continuing to do the work without the missionary there. I have tried over the years to teach the nationals to be decision makers. I am proud of them all. They are real men and women of God. While I was there, there were over forty saved, and for the year of 1987 there were 1,503 professions of faith in Christ.

We had a good furlough, but it was very hard on Don. In every church he'd get up to speak and jokingly say, "I know that Baptists are back patters, but please don't pat me on the back, because I will be out of commission for two or three days." But it was just hard for people not to do this. It would jar his spinal cord and just send shockwaves of electric-like current down his arm. It would take days to get any relief from the pain and would literally take away his strength. When we were with him, we would try and shield him, but it usually didn't work out. He wouldn't let it get him down mentally or emotionally, but physically it was very hard. During the year we were in the States, he was able to lose about forty pounds and finally his diabetes was under control. He knew he had to make some changes in his life if he was going to be able to continue serving the Lord in Argentina, and he was willing to do it. He laughed and said, "Now I only get to eat two-ounce steaks." That was a sacrifice for him, because he loved that great Argentine beef. We started walking every day for exercise and continued doing it when we returned to the field. He felt like God had given him more time to serve Him in Argentina, and he wanted to do anything he had to do to be able to continue preaching and winning souls there.

27

SATAN MEANT IT FOR BAD, BUT GOD MEANT IT FOR GOOD

WHEN GOD IS blessing, we always know that Satan is mad and will try and throw a kink in the works. We'd just been back in the field five weeks, and we had many things going on in the church and with our family too. We were preparing for our daughter Judy's wedding, and everyone was working hard to get everything ready. She was to be married on the fifteenth of July. On the ninth of July, Argentina's Independence Day, we were having a large children's rally in the church to celebrate this very special day. The workers had done all of the planning and were completely in charge of this service. Meanwhile I was busy at home, giving perms and working on things for the wedding. Don was working on his message for the following day. We decided to take a little time and go over to the church to see how the rally was coming along. The following newsletter from Don tells about Satan's attack that day.

AUGUST 1988

When you have been in the Lord's work for over twenty-five years, you are very aware of the existence of Satan. He has fought me, my family, and my work ever since the Lord saved me. I wondered how, when, and where he would strike when we got back to the field. He didn't wait long. Five weeks after our return, he went to work. On the 9th of July, Argentina's Independence Day, we had a special service for children at the church. There were 504 children and some adults with 130 saved including six adults. While we were there one of my neighbors drove up and said, "Get home quick," and then he took off. Arriving at our home we saw two fire trucks, and our house was in flames. The firemen were able to contain the fire to the kitchen and laundry room where we believe it started. But the smoke, heat, and water did extensive damage to the rest of the house.

When we purchased the house nearly eight years ago, the value of the dollar was so low that all we could afford was a house made entirely of adobe—that's right, just dried mud. We live in a very dangerous earthquake zone here next to the Andes Mountains. There have been some killer quakes close to us, but so far none have hit San Rafael very hard since we have been here. Our city is trying to get rid of all the old adobe houses because of the earthquake danger, so it is impossible to get a permit to repair the extensive damage. Because the dollar is very high at this time, we can build a three-bedroom home for about half of what it cost to buy this adobe house eight years ago. I know it's hard to understand that kind of change in the value of money, but here it is a reality.

Don had been concerned for eight years that our house would someday come down on top of us. That adobe was also a breeding place for ants and roaches, so I wasn't too sad to see it torn down, and I was able to have a brand-new home built to our specifications. We did lose a lot of family pictures and needlepoint and cross-stitch pictures the girls and I had worked on together, but they were just material things. We missed them, but it didn't ruin our lives. We lost some of the wedding preparations, and the wedding colors changed from mauve and royal blue to dusty rose and smoky blue, but they still got married on time. We have found throughout the years that laughter is the best medicine, and, believe me, we did a lot of laughing.

A lot of times we think the trials and tragedies of our lives are to hurt us and to discourage us, but God doesn't let anything happen unless it is for our good: **"And we know that all things work together for good to them that love God, to them who are the called according to his purpose." Romans 8:28** has always been a very important scripture in our lives, even when we were single. There were many harder and more serious trials ahead, and we praised God for His Word and the promises in it.

Our house before the fire

Our new house

28

THE WORK GOES FORWARD

DURING 1989, INFLATION began to hit really hard, and people were actually going without food and other needs. The government had provided a box of staples called PAN, but now the government was also broke and stopped this supplement. Don was really burdened for our church families.

In May of that year, Treasure Valley Baptist Church in Meridian, Idaho, gave us a love offering of $14,000. They told Don to use the money however he chose. God put it in Don's heart to help the faithful families of the church by giving them the basic staples they had previously received from the government. There were ten items, and each box cost about $3.50. He would give the number of boxes according to the size of each family. Some received just one box, while others received two or three. He'd also buy vegetables and eggs for them. In a short time, we were helping fifty-three families, and we were able to do this for nearly two years. But each month the cost would go up, until we were paying about three to four times as much for each box than when we had started. These families weren't just so-called "rice Christians," either. They were faithful families that had been coming to the church for a while. The first time we took the boxes to each home, the families were so surprised. It was such a blessing and thrill to see the excitement on their faces. They were so grateful. The inflation went wild during this time, though, and soon the money ran out. We began using our work and personal funds to continue this ministry. When we had to stop delivering the food, we wondered what the reaction of the people would be. Would they be disappointed in us and leave the church? No, they just thanked us over and over again for having helped them through those hard times. It was a tremendous blessing to be part of bringing these people such joy and hope.

In the latter part of 1989, Don began to have problems with his diabetes, and it really became out of control. The doctors in Argentina were giving him injections of steroids to try to help with the pain from his pinched nerve. The steroids caused his diabetes to go up to levels that were really dangerous. With that problem, along with the severe pain from the pinched nerve, he began to lose his strength and was really having a hard time trying to keep going. His hands were numb all the time. He burnt his hand with battery acid and didn't even realize he was burnt until huge blisters come out on his hands. In his newsletter in March 1990, he stated:

> *Please pray for me that I will be able to regain my strength. There is so much to be done down here, and it's been tough. But, thank the Lord for a great group of national workers who have been trained in the work and have carried on the load. They have a wonderful, understanding attitude about my health, and they too are praying for my recovery.*
>
> *God has really blessed this year with 4,408 souls receiving Christ in the three works under our ministry. This is fruit to your account.*

For the next couple of years, Don continued to battle with his health and with the pain, but praise God the work continued to grow, and we started more ministries. We were now averaging close to four hundred each week in San Rafael. We had several big Sundays with over a thousand in attendance and many souls saved. But after a few years of Don's continued health problems and his inability to do all he had done before, the average attendance began to drop down some. We had many Sundays with an attendance of over four hundred, but the average had dropped down to a little more than three hundred. Don was struggling.

In September 1992, we had a new missionary family, Joe and Janis Merlo, come and work with us. They were a tremendous blessing to us and to the work. Joe was willing to do anything we needed him to do, either in the work or in our home. He was Mr. Fix-it, and for the next five years, he kept all of our appliances working.

Don's ministry was changing somewhat. The Lord had lain the desire on his heart to help new missionaries learn the ropes and to try to help them get the best start possible. Joe was such a tremendous blessing because of his attitude. He wanted to learn and had such a humble spirit. He and his family became an intricate part of our work for five years. He was an encouragement to Don during those years because of the way Don's health was deteriorating so quickly. We had been alone out there on the back side of the desert for many years, and now we had the blessing of working with this family.

Since the second year of the ministry, we had held a Bible institute each year, but it was slow with only Don and me teaching as much as we could. Some years later Dante helped with the teaching, but in 1991 we incorporated a four-year Bible institute on video from the ministries of Oremundo, a group out of Texas and Mexico. We were able to use this in all of the works under our ministry. Our son-in-law, Daniel Sanchez, was the head of this ministry for nearly two years. In 1993 Joe took over the leadership of this ministry after Daniel and Judy moved their family to Boise, Idaho. He took the entire burden off of Don of running this and did a great job.

Don was happy that God had given him this new ministry, and we really praised God for Joe and his family, but others who came to work with us were not such a blessing. One couple came with the attitude that the national workers were second-class citizens who didn't know anything about the ministry and administration of carrying on a work. Don gave the man the opportunity of direct-ing the Awana club ministry. His treatment of the national workers was not good. He not only clashed with the workers, but also with the young people in the club. The goal of his wife seemed to be to see how much damage she could do to the ladies and to me. They began to pull some of our sharper young people aside and started having "Bible studies" with them at their home. He confronted Don about some issues he had and would not take any advice Don gave him.

One day it came to a head between him and Don. According to him, Don was just like his own dad, who always thought he was right and everyone else was wrong. He left our church and started a Bible study group in his own home with anyone he could get to come. He was doing much damage in the lives of these young people. They soon left to go to a different city and took several of these young people with them. I am very sorry to say that none of these young people are in church today and have literally lived in the world for the last twenty years. This couple left Argentina after destroying the lives of these young people and the lives of some of the full-time workers in our mission works. What this couple did, took a toll on Don's health, but he wouldn't give up this ministry of trying to help young missionary couples get a good start on the mission field.

Another young couple came who really had a good attitude. The man's attitude was like Joe Merlo's: whatever you want me to do, I'll do it. He wanted to glean and learn from Don and the national pastors. They were a blessing to work with in San Rafael, but a short time later, a church opened up in a different province. The missionary there had to leave the field because of some health issues in his family. This was a good church, but Don knew this young missionary was not ready to pastor a work. He wouldn't listen this time to Don's advice and left a short time afterward. He felt that it was a great opportunity, and it was. Here was an established work, and they already had a nice building and a congregation that needed a pastor. The problem was this couple wasn't ready to take on such a challenge. We went to visit them a short time later, and Don did everything he could to encourage him, but sad to say, they are also out of the ministry now. It wasn't that Don was always right and everyone else was wrong, but God had given him the insight and wisdom to help these new missionaries if they truly wanted to be helped.

29

BE YE STEADFAST

I Corinthians 15:58: "Therefore, my beloved brethren, be ye steadfast, unmovable, always abounding in the work of the Lord, forasmuch as ye know that your labor is not in vain in the Lord."

TIMES WERE GETTING harder financially because of the inflation, but Don was able to continue all of the ministries of the church with the exception of the TV and radio ads and the number of local radio broadcasts that went out each week. But all in all we didn't see much change in attendance or the number of souls saved each week.

One of the men of the church had family in a small town about forty miles west of San Rafael, and he wanted to go with a group to show the film, *The Burning Hell*, in the plaza there. We showed it, and several people made professions of faith, including his family. Don looked into the possibility of starting a work there. This was a very small village, so before he started looking for a building, he sent the workers to ask around about other churches in the area. The workers told Don that there was no gospel-preaching church in this village. Don knew that some of our Bible institute students could do a good job in starting a work here, and it would be a great opportunity to further train these young men. We found an old empty building and rented it for services. We took a busload of people to canvas the town. They passed out tracts and invitations to come and be part of the first service to be held in that building. After that first service, we found out that there was another group of Baptists that had established a work there, and they were very upset about us moving into "their territory." Don wasn't too happy with the workers for not finding out about this Baptist church when they had asked around. He had always been careful not to proselyte any members from other Baptist groups, and he told the workers that they were not to try and recruit anyone from the other church.

For a while things went pretty smoothly; people were getting saved, and the work was growing. We had a mother-daughter tea with a large group of ladies and their daughters. Some of the ladies from San Rafael went to the tea to present a play that we had done at our tea in San Rafael. The ladies that came from San Rafael were so thrilled about having a part in this new work.

Then, one Sunday, no one showed up at all. This was a complete surprise to us. The workers began to ask around to try and find out what had happened. Well, it seems that the Catholic priests had visited every family that was coming and told them they would be condemned to hell if they or their children attended any more services in that "wicked Baptist mission." We went behind the priests, trying to show the people the truth of God's Word, but they had been under the oppression of the Catholic Church for too many years and were very afraid of the condemnation of the Catholic priests. After trying for several weeks to win others and get those new converts back, we decided to stop going out there. We would use our time and workers to try and win another city to Christ. It was our hope that some of the people in this small village might have really meant business with Christ, and they would at least attend the services in the other Baptist work there. Only eternity will tell.

In the early nineties, the government froze the value of the peso. The peso did not change value until late summer of 2001. For many years it was one peso to one dollar. The stability of the peso sounded good, and it was steady. It was the first time it didn't change value two or three times a day, and for the first time in their lives, the people were able to get easy credit and began buying and buying. It was almost a shopping frenzy, but the people did not understand how credit worked. They didn't understand about paying interest on their purchases, and how much that purchase would actually cost them in the end. Things really got out of control. Everyone began buying new color televisions and video players, electric guitars and sound systems, and so on.

It sounded cheap to them, but like I said, they really did not understand how it all worked. All they needed for credit was someone to cosign, so everyone became a cosigner for someone else. Don preached many messages on making good decisions and to be honest in all of your business dealings. He warned them about cosigning and the dangers of it, but this was all so new to them. It just seemed to go in one ear and out the other. We had five full-time workers during this period, and Don told them they should not cosign for anyone. Some listened, but a couple of them didn't. They just trusted their friends to pay. One of the workers cosigned for a neighbor. It wasn't long until he began to get warnings that he would lose everything he owned if he didn't pay what the neighbor owed. It was over $400, and that was a huge amount of money to this worker. The neighbor had moved in the middle of the night with his family and new purchases so excited, leaving the worker to pay for them.

The stability of the peso seemed good for a while, but the prices did not stay the same. Everything was priced in dollars, and the prices kept going higher and higher. The salaries of the people stayed the same during all of this time. They began to miss payments and eventually lost their belongings.

Things became very expensive, and it was difficult to carry on all the different ministries that we had going at the time. Don had to lay off two of the full-time workers and eventually had to cut another worker's hours in half. He hated to do this, but the workers understood the bind we were in at the time. Don always paid the workers a good salary plus all the required benefits. These men did not get mad and leave; they looked for other jobs and started home businesses so they could still work in the ministry. They were good men.

There was something much worse than high prices happening now. Some of the people had so many distractions now that the church became less and less important to them. This was especially true of teenagers. Video game rooms became popular and were another attraction for the teens. The church had been their lives before this phenomenon, because they didn't have any of this before to entertain them. The young people's department took the biggest hit. However, things quickly swung the other way. When the prices started getting higher and higher, people started thinking about God again, because they couldn't pay their bills. It's a shame that a lot of people's love for the Lord is gauged on what He can do for them, or what they need from Him.

Up until 1992, there was way over a thousand who received Christ as their Savior during each year. Now that number began to go down, as it was harder and harder to get unsaved people to hear the Gospel. We continued to follow the calendar of events and would have some large Sundays, and the attendance stayed around two hundred fifty to three hundred.

During this time Don was struggling more and more with his health.

30

MY GRACE IS SUFFICIENT

THE PAIN THAT Don had been enduring in his back and arm for several years was getting worse, to the point where he could no longer function as he wanted. He came to the States to go to Scott White Clinic in Temple, Texas, where they did a series of four nerve blocks in his neck. They went in through the front of his neck to his spine. They thought they would have to put in at least five injections from the front and then five more from the back of his neck. However, after only four of the injections, about 90 percent of the pain was gone. He lost the hypersensitivity in his left arm, and for the first time in many years, he could stand to go without long sleeves or something to cover that arm. He could hardly believe it. He began to feel better and soon had the diabetes under control again. We walked every day to help with this, and it was such a blessing to see that old, enthusiastic Don back. He challenged himself to do better in everything, even in the time it took us to walk around the park each morning. He'd time it and try to cut off a few seconds each day. He was very competitive with himself. He had never lost his desire to win souls and to build a great work for God, but for the first time in years, he was really excited about things again. He felt like our greatest years were yet to come.

For a couple of years, Don was able to go at a pretty good pace, and he was preaching more and more, but he began to notice that his hands were becoming stiff, and there was a lot of numbness in them. They just seemed to be getting weaker all the time. For months he didn't say anything to me about this, but I began to notice that he was having a hard time cutting his meat and his writing was getting harder and harder to read. His penmanship had never been great, but having been a draftsman, he would print most of the time. His printing had always amazed me, because it was so precise. He liked for me to type up his out-lines after he had finished writing them out, but it was getting harder for me to read them. I asked him what was happening, and he told me that for several months he had noticed something was going on with his hands, and they were becoming weaker all the time. We decided it was time to seek out some answers. We booked our flight to the States and outlined everything that we needed the national workers to do in our absence. We had no idea how long we would be gone, but we hoped it would be just for a few weeks. At that time Joe Merlo was on a furlough, so we left the work completely in the hands of the national workers. The following is from a newsletter that Don sent out to our sup-porting pastors:

URGENT PRAYER NEEDED!

June 1996

Greetings Brethren! I thank you for your faithful prayers over the years. I'm sure they are what have sustained my family and me in Argentina for over twenty-one years through the dangers and trials we have faced.

Now I urgently need your prayers once again. For the last few years my physical strength has been slowly deteriorating due to the car accident that I had fifteen years ago. Right now it even hurts me to pick up anything over two or three pounds. I've lost control of several of my fingers and have constant pain and numbness in my hands and arms. I had an MRI scan taken a few weeks ago, and the results show that I have several cavities called syrinxes on my spinal cord. They are filled with fluid and putting pressure on my nervous system and are killing the nerves to my hands and arms. If it is not operated on, it will eventually leave me completely paralyzed. My understanding is that they will try and cover up the opening in the base of the brain from which the fluid is draining out. The cavities will then dry up on their own. It is a very delicate operation, and the doctors say they will only have one shot at it, whatever that means. At this time, everything points to it being done at Barnes Hospital in St. Louis, Missouri. Please pray that the operation will be a success, and I will regain my strength to continue the ministry that God has called me to in western Argentina.

The purpose of this operation was not to restore what he had lost but to actually slow down the progress of the paralysis. The prognosis was that he would be totally paralyzed on down the line, but this surgery was to prolong his mobility. When they did the surgery, it was very different from what they said they were going to do. They went into his spinal cord and put a stint in place at the seventh cervical vertebra to drain off the fluids so the syrinxes would dry up. They said it was a much easier surgery for him, but in reality, it was a very hard surgery for him to go through. He was in intensive care for several days and was in extreme pain. He could not take morphine, because it would cause him to have terrible hallucinations. There are, of course, other pain killers, but it seemed as if nothing would help alleviate the pain. Don was not a complainer, but I could read his face, and I knew when it was getting worse. If I asked him if it was really bad, he would shake his head yes. When he began to come out of it and they moved him to a private room, we began to realize how very weak he was (although, in comparison to later surgeries, he was doing well). The following is part of his newsletter a month after the surgery:

> *The doctors told me that I may need a second surgery if the syrinxes didn't drain and dry up. Please KEEP PRAYING! There was a lot of pain involved, and as you can imagine, I don't want to go through this again. Although, I have always found that God's Grace is sufficient. I trust Him completely for whatever the future holds, because it's all in His all-powerful hands.*

Some strange things began to take place in his body after the surgery. He lost 50 percent of his hearing in his right ear, which he later recovered, but another more serious and painful thing happened. Before the surgery all the numbness and pain was from his waist up, but now he also had numbness in his hips and his left leg and foot, and his knees became very stiff. It was extremely uncomfortable, but he said it was not too painful. He sent out a newsletter to our supporting churches asking for more prayer and also to tell them that we had planned to return to Argentina in November, but that didn't happen.

The whole objective of the surgery was to stop the progression of the paralysis. The doctors in the hospital ordered more tests. A different doctor came with the results in his hand to talk to Don and me. This doctor said he had met with six other neurosurgeons, and they agreed they could not do anything else to help him. He said that the spinal cord had grown to the fusion in Don's neck, and it would be impossible to separate them without completely paralyzing him. They hoped that some of the numbness would subside, but for now he would have to live with this. They had done all they could.

We stayed in a mission apartment for a couple of months until Don had recuperated some of his strength back. They had started him on physical therapy while in the hospital, so we continued doing that until he could walk again without help. However, we knew that he was in no condition to return to the field. We moved to a mission house in Springfield, Missouri, to give him more time to recuperate.

While in Springfield, one of our former pastors advised Don to try and get into the Mayo Clinic in Rochester, Minnesota. It usually takes several months to get an appointment, but one week after we called them, there was a cancellation. We jumped at the opportunity to see a specialist in spinal cord injuries there during the Thanksgiving holidays. We were very nervous about this appointment but hopeful they could do something more for Don. After many tests and examinations, they came to the same conclusion as the doctors in Saint Louis, Missouri. There was nothing they could do to help him. The doctor looked at him and said, "You will have to be satisfied with what movement you have, because in reality, you should have been paralyzed for life. It would be absolutely too risky to try and operate again." He compared Don's injuries to that of Christopher Reeve's spinal cord injury and told us that Don should have been in the same physical condition for the rest of his life.

When we left, we had mixed emotions. We had hoped that they could help him, but we rejoiced once again in the miracle that God had performed in Don's body after our car wreck in 1981. In a newsletter dated January 1997, Don wrote:

*Since our trip to Mayo Clinic, I seem to be getting weaker in my knees and legs, and my hands don't seem to want to function correctly, but we've decided to go back to the field and continue working there for my Lord. Please pray for strength to do God's work. II Corinthians 12:9, 10: "And he said unto me, my grace is sufficient for thee: for my strength is made perfect in weakness. Most gladly therefore will I rather glory in my infirmities, that the power of Christ may rest upon me. Therefore, I take pleasure in infirmities, in reproaches, in necessities, in persecutions, in distresses for Christ's sake: **for when I am weak, then am I strong.**"*

31

I CAN DO ALL THINGS THROUGH CHRIST

Don continued to work with a team of physical therapists after we returned to Argentina, but his strength began to decline. He didn't have the strength to stand and preach anymore. The national workers understood, so they continued on as they had while we were gone. Carlos Cejas taught the adults and was in charge of the Awana Club and the visitation program. Luis Yañez continued working with the young people and taking care of the Bible institute. He also took turns with Carlos preaching Sunday evenings. Although Don could not preach and do the things he had done before, they were happy to have their pastor back.

We moved his office downstairs because he could no longer climb the stairs. He really enjoyed being back in his office with his "friends," which he loving called his books. After breakfast he'd go to his office and study and pray and listen to preaching tapes that were sent from churches in the States. The following is an excerpt from his newsletter in July of 1997:

I appreciate your prayers for me concerning my health and the work. In my last newsletter I told you how weak I was, and it does not seem to be getting better. In May I had another MRI, and they said that I have spinal fluid collecting in my brain. The doctor told me this could very well be the reason for the continuing weakness. He also stated that if I keep getting weaker, they may have to do another surgery but this time on my brain to drain the fluid off of it. Please continue to pray.

However, I am praising the Lord that I was able to preach for the first time in four months. I had to do it sitting on a high stool. It sure wasn't the same and it was way out of style for me, but God blessed His Word and we had a great service. You should have seen the joy on the faces of the people when I told them to open their Bibles and I began to preach. This was an answer to their faithful prayers for their missionary.

We are so grateful for our workers who are doing the biggest share of the work here in San Rafael and in our other three works. It has been a joy to train these people to do the Lord's work, but it's a greater joy to see them carrying it out.

Since Don could not go out much, he began to teach disciple-ship classes in our home. He had asked for prayer for our physical therapists: a man, his wife, and their assistant. We had been witnessing to them at each session of therapy. Don led the husband to the Lord and continued to witness to his wife, who was a very staunch Catholic. She was also a teacher of catechism in a large Catholic church. Don gave her some information about the Ten Commandments in the catechism book and in her own Catholic Bible. They were not the same. She was very angry at having been deceived for so many years. We invited her and her husband to come to our house for Bible study. She was gloriously saved the very first week. Don then began to disciple both of them, and they started coming faithfully to church. I had the privilege of winning the assistant to Christ, and she began to bring her family to church. One of her sisters is now a pastor's wife, married to one of Carlos Cejas's sons.

God just kept giving new ways Don could continue to serve Him even though he was very weak. Sadly his health began to deteriorate rapidly. In late August 1997, we decided to go to Houston, Texas, where some of the world's best doctors were practicing. Pastor Larry Maddox in Houston told us that he was very good friends with one of the best neurosurgeons, and he would get us in to see him. We knew this was the right thing to do. In September 1997, after many tests and examinations, the doctor operated on Don's brain and inserted a VP value in the left side of his brain with a shunt that drained the fluid down into his stomach area. This was another very painful surgery, but the results were great. All of the numbness and stiffness left his lower body, but he had to learn to walk again. This was now the third time he had learned to walk. He would push himself in his physical therapy sessions to the point that he just couldn't do another thing. He had to use a wheelchair for several weeks until he had enough strength in his legs again to be able to walk without assistance. He would not give up trying to be independent again.

After a few months, we returned to Argentina. He continued with the ministries that God had given him, teaching discipleship classes in our home, and another ministry was added. Don had never done much personal counseling; he tried to do most of it from the pulpit in his messages. Since he could no longer do much preaching, he began to counsel individually in his home office. This took a toll on him, both emotionally and physically.

As before, we tried walking every day in the park to help keep his diabetes under control, but after a few months, he began to walk sideways. We first thought it might have been due to his blood sugar levels dropping, but testing showed the levels were fine. We called his neurosurgeon in Houston, and he told us to have the VP value checked to see if it was pumping all right. We did this, and it proved to be functioning perfectly. The surgeon in Houston told us that something else much more serious had to be going on, and we needed to come back to Houston.

The MRI and CAT scan showed that a second series of syrinxes had developed in Don's spinal cord that went all the way down to the T-3 vertebra. The T-4 vertebra controls the respiratory system. The doctor explained that going into the spinal cord one time was very dangerous, but going into it a second time was extremely delicate and dangerous. He told us that he had no idea how Don's body would react to the surgery if he put another shunt in at the T-3, but without the surgery he would have only a matter of weeks before he would be totally paralyzed for the rest of his life. I didn't want Don to go through another critical surgery again, but after praying about it for several hours, he decided he would do it if there was a possibility that there would be a longer period of time before I had to completely take care of him.

Our daughter Judy and son John flew to Texas to be with us. When Don came out of surgery, he looked so pale and feeble. I didn't know what to expect, and when I saw him, I wondered if he would survive this invasion into his nervous system. He was in intensive care only a couple of days, and then he was moved to a private room. He wanted to read a newspaper, and John handed it to him. Don was so weak that paper slipped right through his fingers. Then all of a sudden, his legs began to spasm, and he looked terrified. This was just exactly what the doctor had meant. They had no idea how Don's body would react to all of this.

John and Judy were really shaken up after seeing their dad in this condition. They both had to fly out the next day with that image in their minds, but his body began to calm down. The physical therapists took over, trying to teach him once again to walk, to keep his balance, and to regain some strength. A few days later, the therapist was walking with him, and Don's ankle gave out, causing his foot to turn the wrong way. He broke the lower leg bone. This really set him back, but they continued to do what they could with him. The occupational therapist worked with his hands to retrain them to work together and to become stronger. He could no longer write at all with his right hand, so they tried to train his left hand to take over. He worked very hard at all of this, but this time it took more than a year to recuperate. In that time, he went from not being able to stand by himself to walking with a walker and then with a cane.

The following is from a newsletter dated August 1999:

> I want to thank you all for your prayers about my health. Please continue! I've been in therapy for the last 10 months. I've gone from not being able to walk by myself to walking short distances with a cane. I couldn't eat by myself or actually do anything alone. I still need help to dress and bathe, but I can eat by myself and do much more than the doctor thought was possible. I've even had the privilege of preaching God's Word four times in the past month. I have to sit at a table and preach, but my wife said that I don't sound any different now than when I was running around the platform. So this is a tremendous encouragement as it has been two years since I had the strength to preach at all.
>
> By the Grace of God we will be heading back to Argentina at the end of September. I may end up in a wheelchair all the time, but the way I look at it, I can serve the Lord in a wheelchair in Argentina as well as here in the States.

We were very happy and ready to go back and continue working on the field. Although Don knew there would be a lot of challenges that he would have to face going back to Argentina, he believed that God was not through with him yet. His attitude was the same as the Apostle Paul when he wrote in Philippians 4:13: **"I can do all things through Christ which strengthened me."**

32

A LIVE DOG IS BETTER THAN A DEAD LION

We thought we were going home in September, but three days before we were to leave, Don had a grand mal seizure. It was the third one that he'd had in fifteen years. It lasted several minutes and was so severe that it really did a lot of damage to his body. His spine was badly shaken. The seizure caused a lot more numbness and took away a lot of Don's strength that he had worked so hard to regain. For the next two and a half months, we went back to therapy to try and help him get stronger. He could no longer walk with a cane and never reached that point again. He could walk short distances with his walker, but now he was confined mostly to his wheelchair. The following is from a newsletter written in December 1999:

PRAISE GOD WE'RE GOING HOME!
The Lord willing we will be leaving Miami the 7th of December heading
for our home in San Rafael, Mendoza, Argentina, where we have had

the privilege of serving the Lord for the last twenty-five years. We have been in the States for fourteen months because of medical problems. We want to thank everyone for their prayers for my health, for my family, and for the work in Argentina.

Most of you know from my newsletters that in the last three years I have had two operations on my spinal cord and one brain surgery. I have gotten progressively worse, but I still believe the Scripture in **Ecclesiastes 9:4: "A living dog is better than a dead lion."** *By the Grace of God I'm still alive. Now much of my time I'm confined to a wheelchair, but praise the Lord, my voice and my mind are still there, and I have been able to preach several times. This was done, of course, sitting in my wheelchair and sitting at a table. I have found out that you don't have to romp and spit and snort or run all over the platform to get your message across. So please pray for me as we go back to the field that I will be able to teach and to preach more of God's Word and God's will to the precious people in Argentina. I'm excited about being able to go back to our work there.*

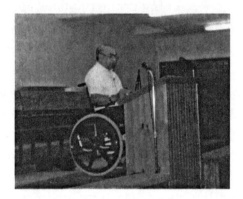

As soon as we arrived back in San Rafael, the men of the church went to work building a ramp and a pulpit that would accommodate Don's wheelchair. They built it exactly the right height for Don to be able to see his message clearly. When we would arrive at church, there was always someone waiting to help me lift Don out of the truck, and they loved taking him into the auditorium. Whatever they could do to make their pastor comfortable was a joy to them. When it was time for him to preach, there was always a group of men prepared to change out the pulpit, locate the ramp, and get him onto the platform. It took just a couple of minutes to get him ready to preach.

Mornings were difficult for Don, so he had Carlos Cejas continue to teach and preach in the Sunday morning service, but he would preach each Sunday night. The joy among the people was precious to see; their pastor was behind his pulpit once again to preach the Word of God. Normally he could barely lift his arms up because of the nerve damage, but once he started preaching, his right arm would go up in the air when he was trying to make a gesture to get a point across. He didn't even realize this was happening, but the people picked up on it right away. They would comment on his message and say, "Did you see how many times the pastor raised his arm up tonight?" It was almost like they gauged the power of the message on how many times that arm would fly up in the air.

God was blessing the church, and it began to really grow again. The attendance had not lowered much in our absence, but we could see that the people were excited again about working for the Lord. We were seeing more and more people come and receive Christ as their Savior. Don was really happy being back, but there were times when he really struggled with his disabilities. He wanted to do so much more than was possible for him. It would take him two or three days to recuperate his strength after preaching a message, but he wasn't going to let this stop him.

From the time of the brain surgery, Don had to sleep in a recliner. When he tried to sleep in a bed, his legs would hurt too badly. Every night we would struggle to get his legs raised to just the right height and cushion them so there was the least amount of pressure on them possible. He was always in pain, but he never complained about it. By this time he needed my assistance with just about everything he had to do, but it was great to see him this happy again. We settled into a routine each day, and his care became easier as we learned how to work together in accomplishing the different tasks that he had always done by himself. Although I still worked some with the national pastors on different projects, my main concern now was the care of my husband.

During the next three years, we encountered some problems with some of the workers in the church, and this was very hard on Don emotionally. There were times when he really struggled to keep going, but he'd laugh and say, "A living dog is better than a dead lion." We would still go out and eat once in a while, and this always caused a stir in the restaurants. In San Rafael it was rare to see someone in a wheelchair out in public. They just stayed hidden in their homes; therefore, there were very few places that were wheelchair accessible. The waiters in the restaurants would come to help me lift Don's wheelchair up a couple of steps to the dining area, and they would try to help us to a table that was best suited for his needs. We actually became accustomed to people staring at us all the time. One of the more difficult things was pushing him along the sidewalks. They are all made of tile and are very uneven. I learned how to navigate them, but we did this as little as possible.

During that three-year period, we had a couple of setbacks but nothing too serious. Things were looking up, and we thought that God was actually going to let us stay there for a long time. It was Don's desire for the Lord to take him home to heaven from Argentina. He said, "I would rather preach out, than burn out." He prayed that God would never stop using him to win souls and to preach, and it seemed like God was pouring out His power on Don's preaching. We were seeing lives changed and souls saved nearly every week. We were truly happy in our service there. We couldn't do all that we had done before, but we were there doing what we could.

The first Sunday night in May 2001, Don was preaching a message from **James 1:22: "Be ye doers of the Word and not hearers only..."** It seemed as if God had poured out His spirit on Don that night. The people responded to the message, and the altars were full. Don was exhausted after he preached but very happy. That night he said, "I will be a happy man if the Lord just lets me keep on preaching," but that was the last time he ever preached in Argentina.

33

WE KNOW THAT ALL THINGS
WORK TOGETHER FOR GOOD

GOD SAYS IN **Romans 8:28, "And we know that all things work together for good to them that love God, to them who are the called according to *His* purpose."** This scripture has always been our family's life verse. Our kids heard it over and over through the years, and each has it memorized.

In reading of the trials and health struggles that Don and our family went through, one might be asking, how in the world can that be true? God had proven himself over and over to us. We did not always (we usually didn't) know what the reason or purpose was for the trials, but we knew that God was in control of the situation, and as Don always said, "This wasn't a surprise to God!" Don always tried to reinforce in all of us and in our church family that whatever God was doing, it was for our good. However, the greatest trial yet was just now starting.

After preaching that wonderful message on Sunday night, May 6, 2001, Don was physically exhausted. He slept off and on all day Monday and most of Tuesday. I was not too surprised when he was so tired that he barely felt like eating. He knew he had to, though, to keep his blood sugar from dropping too low. He still did not feel like going out to church on Wednesday night. Thursday morning I needed to go downtown to pick up a few things. A girl from our church was helping me in the house, so I asked her to look in on him a couple of times after I left. I fixed his breakfast and sat it on the tray in front of his recliner. I was a little nervous about leaving him that morning, because he still seemed exhausted and a little lethargic. When I came back, he still hadn't touched his breakfast and was just sitting there, staring at the television. I asked him a question, and he didn't seem to understand what I asked. I called for an ambulance service, which was their equivalent to our 911 calls. They came right away and took his blood pressure, which was high. His blood sugars were also high. They said he probably was having an episode with his diabetes. I just wasn't too sure they knew what they were talking about, so I called his neurosurgeon in Fort Worth, Texas. He told me to once again have the neurologist come and check his VP value to see if it was pumping regularly.

He came and tested it. He said that it did not seem to be functioning properly. He told me to manually pump it every fifteen minutes, all night long, and then we would see in the morning how he was doing. It did not help, and by Friday morning, I was sure that it was a stroke. That was one thing I had not even thought about until now, and I did not know exactly how to check for it. I again called the doctor in Texas, and he said he had come to the same conclusion and that I needed to get Don in to have an MRI as quickly as possible. Well, the soonest available time was Saturday morning. Now, this was all being done under the supervision of the "best" neurologist in San Rafael. He came to the house several times Friday and Saturday to check on Don.

Saturday morning the MRI was done. After they finished the MRI, the technician left. We waited all morning for the results, but nothing happened. The man had left to go on a vacation without leaving the results with the doctor. Believe it or not, this is all true. The doctor called all over the country until he located this technician. The MRI showed that Don had had a massive stroke in the left side of his brain. The doctor called the ambulance and they took us to the hospital, but the damage was already done. They put an IV in his arm and started giving him the medicine to reverse the effects of the stroke, but it was forty-eight hours too late. Don did not have any idea what was going on. Our pastors brought his recliner to the hospital for him to sleep in that night. You have to have someone stay all the time with the patient in most of the hospitals in Argentina. This person has to do all of the care of the patient other than administer the medication. Since I was not familiar with the effects of a stroke, I tried to feed Don the food they brought to the room. He would open his mouth but could not chew or swallow the food. It would just fall out of his mouth. We had a very difficult night, and things just seemed to be getting worse.

On Sunday afternoon after the morning service, about forty people from the church came to see Don and pray for him. He seemed to know the people but had no idea what was happening. The men stayed in his room and prayed for him, and I went out into the hall to pray and talk to the women. After seeing their pastor in this condition, they were all crying and praying. It was a precious moment, seeing the love they had for Don. This was the last time they would ever see their pastor.

The men of the church decided that I needed someone to stay with me to help me lift him to take care of his needs. From that moment on, until we flew out of Argentina on May 26, one of the men of the church was with me constantly.

Meanwhile, our mission office was trying to get an air ambulance into San Rafael to fly him to Houston, but things move very slowly down there. There are always many complications when dealing with the governments, and flying through the air space of different countries, and also in dealing with the customs agents.

On Sunday night Don had another grand mal seizure. Praise God the young man who stayed that night was able to help me to keep Don from hurting himself any worse than he already was. It took the doctors a half hour to get enough medicine in him to stop the seizure. We'll never know how much more damage was done to his brain that night. After six days they sent Don home because they couldn't do anything else to help him. Two of our daughters, Judy and Shelley, flew down to be with their dad. Anna was already in Argentina and went through all of this with him. Seeing their dad in this condition took an emotional toll on all three of the girls.

On May 26, 2001, the air ambulance landed in San Rafael. Don and I went in the ambulance to the airport. Our national pastors all came out with their families to see us off. Don still had no idea what was going on at the moment. The minute they carried him onto the plane, they began to hook him up with all the necessary equipment to keep him alive. The doctor on the plane said that if we had been delayed just another hour or two, Don would have died from kidney failure. God was still looking out for his servant. The flight took fourteen hours. We were met in Houston by another ambulance and taken to St. Luke's Medical Center. Our doctor was there to meet us. After examining him and reading what had been done to him in San Rafael, the doctor looked at me and said, "I can't believe he has survived all of this. He must have a tremendous will to live."

The following is an article that our daughter, Shelley, wrote for the *Osborne County Farmers* about her dad.

My Dad Is, And Always Will Be, My Hero

Father's Day is only a couple of weeks away, so I thought I'd tell you about my Dad, who happens to be an awesome guy. Growing up, I thought he was the strongest man in the world. We would all jump on his back, trying to knock him down. We would wrestle with him, play ball with him, and go fishing with him. He was like Superman to me. Then twenty years ago, that all changed in one terrible instant when my parents and younger brother and sister were in a car accident. This happened in Argentina where my folks are missionaries. The doctors told us we'd probably be orphans by morning. Wow, talk about tact! Thank God they didn't die, but my Dad's neck was broken and he became Superman to me in a different way.

Over the years I have watched him go through surgery after surgery and saw his determination as he had to relearn to do everything—more than once. Through all of this I rarely heard him complain, even when a small sneeze caused him terrible pain. It is from my Dad that I have learned to take what life throws at you and find the joy and humor in it. He has gradually been losing mobility and has had to use a wheelchair quite a bit in the last few years, but he has never stopped laughing and making faces; he's never given up; he's never stopped serving God.

My Mom called last month and told us my Dad had suffered a massive stroke. I found myself on a plane a few days later, on my way to Argentina, to be with the man who taught me so many things. I was afraid of what I would find, afraid he would no longer be the man I spent hours fishing with and the man who laughed at all my corny jokes. What I found was a man who, though totally paralyzed on the right side of his body, was trying to cheer people up by making faces with the left side of his face. I found a man who could barely talk, but let us know that he loved us very much.

My Dad is now in Houston in the hospital, he was flown out of Argentina in a Lear Jet Air Ambulance, and the doctors aren't sure yet what the outcome of all this will be. But whatever happens, <u>my Dad is, and always will be, my hero,</u> the sort of man legends should be written about. I love you, Dad.

34

NOT MURPHY'S LAW BUT GOD'S GRACE

MURPHY'S LAW SAYS anything that can go wrong, will go wrong. Don always added this to Murphy's Law: "So don't get too shook up or excited over it." We usually tried to have a plan A, B, C, and so on. I believe I mentioned in one of the earlier chapters that our kids really thought we lived by Murphy's Law. (Actually, they started calling it the "Espinosa Curse.")

We stayed at St. Luke's for two weeks. The doctor said that Don was completely aphasic, which meant that his brain was completely jumbled up. It was going to be the job of the therapists to try and put it back in order. He was now completely paralyzed on his right side, and his left side was so weak from the spinal cord problems that he could no longer use it either, or even begin to know how to use it. After a few days of clinical examinations and more MRIs, MRAs, and CT scans, they said he was out of danger from the massive stroke but that he could have another one at any time. The doctor told me that the right side of his brain had been severely damaged, but they would try and work with him to see what they could help him recuperate, cognitively and physically. They said that most progress would be in the first six months, and after that the percentage would go down with each month. He would also have to be on a completely liquid diet, because his tongue and throat muscles were paralyzed. When I thought about the food they had given him in San Rafael—how it would only roll out of his mouth, and how he would choke with each sip of liquid—I understood why and thought how merciful the Lord was to have kept him from choking to death. The other danger was that the food and liquids could have gone into his lungs and caused pneumonia. We had so many things to praise the Lord for at that time.

They started him on speech therapy a couple days later. He had absolutely no ability to tell you what a clock was or was used for, or a spoon, or even a toothbrush. He could read words but could not even begin to match a word with an object.

The first week in Houston was very hard for me, because I felt as if I had not only lost my husband but my best friend. He couldn't remember my name and would always call me by his sister's name. I stayed with him in the hospital room all the time. He seemed to be terrified when I would leave for a few minutes. He began to cry a lot, and this tore my heart out. My upbeat husband, who had always been very protective of me and had always treated me like a queen, was now helpless and terrified. It seemed as if he didn't think anyone would know what he needed except for me, because he could not tell them.

There were some strange things, though, that were happening. Although it was very difficult to understand him, when one of his pastor friends would call, he could speak spontaneously to them, but if they asked him something that he had to think about, he was lost. I was so grateful to Pastor Billy Sharp and his wife, Gerri, for their visits and for the advice and counseling that Gerri was able to share with me, especially about being a full-time care giver. There were many pastors in the area who came to see and encourage us. I praise God for each one of them.

Now, back to Murphy's Law! During the weekend of the second week of June, there was a hurricane that hit Houston full force. The hospital lost electricity right at the beginning of the storm, but of course the backup generators took over. The staff immediately evacuated all of the patients on life support and the critically ill patients. After a few hours, the basement of the hospital flooded and the generators failed. At the time we had raised Don's bed up high to make it easier to take care of his needs. When they lost electricity, we could not get the bed down to a level where we could safely transfer Don. For three days and two nights, we were without electricity, water, or air. All of the elevators were down, and we were on the seventeenth floor. The workers would carry gallons of water up each flight to use for drinking, bathing, and other needs, but it was impossible to bring up enough to take care of all the needs. Things became pretty raunchy after three days. They would carry up sandwiches from a sandwich shop and canned liquids for those who could not swallow.

However, God even used that situation for our good. The doctor had been trying to get Don into a rehab hospital, but they did not have any beds available on the stroke floor. Guess where we were evacuated to? To that very rehab hospital. They put Don on the children's floor, and there we stayed for two or three weeks until there was a bed open on the stroke floor. They worked and worked with Don, but he was not making much progress at all. Every little sign of progress was a cause for celebration.

I said in one of the earlier chapters how close Don and his sister had been growing up. During our stay in Houston, she flew in from California to be with him. She was heartsick when she tried to talk to Don, and he could not answer back. Don had witnessed to his sister for nearly forty years, but her answer had always been "when I'm ready." She was very angry at God when she saw her brother's condition. Her question was, how could God let all this happen to her brother, who was always trying to help others? After two weeks she returned to California.

After six more weeks, we finally had to make a decision about where to go after the rehab hospital. I must confess that I was scared to death. For the first time in my thirty-eight years of marriage, I had to make all of the decisions. I talked to a counselor about the decisions ahead, and I knew that somehow God was going to lead me to make the right one. After talking to her, I at least had an idea of what to expect.

I decided the best decision was to have Don transferred to Springfield, Missouri. Since Springfield was where our mission board was located, there were always missionaries coming and going. I thought it would be good for Don to be where old friends could come and see him.

I called our friend, Pastor Dick Webster, and asked him to try and locate a wheelchair-accessible van for us. He did this, and it was such a tremendous blessing. He and his son-in-law drove it to Houston to pick us up and drive us to Springfield. We were going to stay the weekend in Lewisville, Texas, where Dick pastored. The van was a full-size conversion van with a lift installed. We managed to get Don in the van, and we tried to transfer him out of the wheelchair onto the back seat. His foot caught between our feet, and when we turned him, it broke his leg. We thought his ankle was just sprained, so we decided to go ahead and drive to Lewisville. We bought some ice, and I sat on the floor in front of him holding the ice on his foot, trying to keep his foot from being jarred during our trip. By the time we arrived in Lewisville, he was in horrible pain. We took him to a hospital, and sure enough, his leg was broken. This was the same bone that had been broken in the hospital after his last surgery. They stabilized it with a boot and said we would need to get it put in a cast when we arrived in Springfield. I was very glad when we finally arrived there, but that joy didn't last very long.

When we arrived at the nursing facility and Don saw where we were, he looked terrified. The social worker assured him that he would be on a special wing just for rehab patients. This was the beginning of three very hard weeks for him. Because his leg was now in a plaster cast, they held off on some of his physical therapy, but they decided to start him on occupational therapy right away. At the rehab hospital in Houston, all of the therapists had written in a notebook what therapy had been done with Don and what his range of motion and his abilities were at that point. He had a very limited range of motion in his right shoulder and arm. The occupational therapist at the nursing home would not look at the notebook at all. He said he knew just what Don needed. He came into the room, took Don's right arm in his hand, and lifted it up over Don's head. Don screamed out in pain and told the man to leave. That mistake caused him severe pain that lasted for several years. He was miserable and kept asking me to get him out of that place.

I stayed with Don every day until he took an afternoon nap. I would then leave for a couple of hours to look for a place to live. It took three weeks, but I finally found a wheelchair-accessible house. God was so good to us in giving us a home that took care of all of our needs. Medicare took care of getting all the necessary equipment that I needed to take care of Don. God was not only taking care of Don's needs, but He was looking after me too. The equipment was top of the line and easy to use.

For the next six months, we were on a home health care program. The therapists, doctor, nurses, came in at different times. Someone else came to help me bathe him. We again settled into a schedule, and Don was beginning to improve little by little. I became more confident in taking care of him and learned how to do it without hurting him or myself.

After a couple of months, Don wanted to try and go to church. At first it was very hard on him. By the time I had him dressed and ready to go, he was exhausted. Many times we would get to the church and turn around and go back home, because he knew that he would not be able to sit through a service. We both missed being in the Lord's house on Sundays, but when we couldn't attend, we would watch a service on TV.

After six months Don wanted to start going out for therapy. He had by then lost over fifty pounds. It was much easier on me to take care of him, but I was worried because he was barely eating enough to keep him from being malnourished. The doctor wanted to locate a feeding tube, but Don would not hear of it. When we started going out for therapy, he decided he wanted to go to a restaurant to eat. They had been training him to learn to swallow again by doing exercises with his tongue and throat. The first restaurant we went to was a Chinese one. He wanted sweet and sour shrimp. By taking tiny bites, he was able to eat one piece, and he was through. It wore him out, but he wouldn't give up. The next time we tried Italian, and that worked a little better. He really enjoyed going out, because it seemed almost like a normal thing to do.

We stayed in Springfield for one year. In that year he lost over one hundred pounds and looked so gaunt and old, but he never gave up trying to get stronger and to speak more clearly. He was always playful with the therapists, and they loved working with him. He'd do the best he could to witness to them, but it was very hard for him to find words when he tried to talk. However, he wouldn't give up trying.

During our one-year stay, he insisted that we would someday go back to Argentina. He had not lost his long-term memory, and he still loved Argentina with all his heart.

35

NONE OF THESE THINGS SHALL MOVE ME

WHEN DON WAS able to go out to therapy, he liked to stop by the mission office once in a while. He would go in and talk to Dr. Bob Baird, who was our mission director at the time. Don kept telling him over and over that we were going back to Argentina soon. Dr. Baird knew in his heart that it was not likely that we would be going back, but he would encourage Don to keep on getting better. During the year in Springfield, Don was in the hospital several times with pneumonia, bladder infections, and bronchitis.

On October 4, 2001, Don's sister came for another visit. Don still could not say much to her, but one evening she came into his room and said, "Don, I'm ready to get saved." Don looked at her, and all he was able to say was "You know what to do; just do it." She prayed and asked the Lord to forgive her and come into her heart. They both cried and hugged each other and called me into the room. Dolores said through her tears, "Don just put Jesus in my heart." Don laughed and shook his head and just replied, "Jesus." Although he couldn't express what he wanted to say, he certainly knew what had just taken place. After forty years, Dolores had been gloriously saved.

Years ago Don preached a message entitled, "None of These Things Shall Move Me." The scripture is **Acts 20:24: "But none of these things move me, neither count I my life dear unto myself, so that I might finish my course with joy, and the ministry, which I have received of the Lord Jesus, to testify the gospel of the grace of God."** This scripture described my husband. He had one desire, and that was to finish the course that God had set before him and to finish it with joy. Even through all the trials and sufferings, he still wasn't going to let any of these things move him away from his course.

Our daughter, Anna, was with us most of our stay in Springfield. She was offered a job to work full-time in a church ministry in Ohio. We encouraged her to take it, because we knew how much she wanted to serve the Lord. After she had left, I knew that soon we would have to decide what our next step was going to be. In Don's mind and heart, we were still going back to Argentina, but meanwhile, I needed to be someplace where our other children would be available to help out once in a while. Our daughter, Judy, and her husband offered to put us on a plane to Boise, Idaho, where they and our daughter, Donna, lived. After we left, they would then finish packing up our house and drive our van pulling a trailer to Boise.

Don already loved Boise because it looked so much like San Rafael and the area around it. We were very familiar with the church, and we knew the pastor there. We would also be with two of our kids and five of our grandkids. In September we started this new chapter in our lives.

Through different circumstances two more of our kids moved to the area to be close to their dad and to go to our church. John and his family came from Florida in June 2003, and Anna and her husband came from Ohio in 2006. We now had four of our children and seven grandchildren there. Shelley and her family lived in Osborne, Kansas, where he pastors a church. They were able to come up to see us three or four times through the years. Don loved to have all the grandkids around him. Sometimes he would get a little nervous, and I would have to get him in bed to rest, but he was happy they were there.

When we arrived in Boise, we immediately started with new therapists. Don still had such a hard time finding words, but he kept working. They just couldn't seem to make a breakthrough in unscrambling his mind. The speech therapists began to try to help him read sentences in a way that others could understand him.

In 2004, we were invited to three different mission conferences. One conference was in California, one was in Texas, and one was at our home church here in Meridian, Idaho. The therapist had me type out Don's testimony and began working with him so he could read it in a way it could be understood and loud enough that a microphone could pick it up. Five minutes was the maximum time he could read. It would exhaust him to the point where his mind would just literally shut down.

The conference in California was in February 2004. Don was really happy to be in the church where he had preached their mission conference for twelve years. They just wanted to honor him and love on him. It was a precious time. Some of our church family from Long Beach, California, came to visit us during this conference. Don had led each one of them personally to the Lord. We had wonderful fellowship with them.

By the time we flew to Texas in October, he was able to read a longer testimony. Both of these conferences were such an encouragement to him. He still wanted to go back to Argentina, but he knew by this time it just wasn't going to be possible. As in

Springfield, he had been in the hospital several times because of infections and pneumonia. He just wasn't physically strong enough to cope with the travel and hardships of the field. We officially took a medical retirement in March 2004. Don was sad, because he missed the people and the work so much, but he knew it was the right thing to do.

On the twenty-fourth of October, 2004, our church here in Idaho wanted to honor Don during the mission conference. It was absolutely an incredible night. Our daughter, Anna, and her husband had flown in from Ohio, supposedly on their vacation, and our daughter, Shelley, flew in from Osborne, Kansas, surprising us. It was the first time that all five of our kids had been together in seventeen years.

The service started with a PowerPoint presentation of our lives that Judy had put together. Then they called Don and me up on the platform. Of course, Don was in his wheelchair and our son, grandson, and sons-in-law carried him up the stairs. After seeing the presentation and the live footage of our four national pastors, we were pretty emotional.

Don had his testimony ready to read, and through many tears he managed to read it. There was not a dry eye in the auditorium of around six hundred people. After Don's testimony, Pastor DeMichele stood up, looked at us, and said, "Don and Cherie, we know that you are unable to return to Argentina, so we thought we would bring a little bit of Argentina to you." In walked our four national pastors: Carlos Cejas, Luis Yañez, Dante Garcia, and Ricardo Orozco. Pastor DeMichele and our children had been so concerned about how Don would take this surprise that they actually had our doctor sitting in the front row just in case Don needed him. Pastor DeMichele, Pastor Randy Mitchell, and our children had worked together for six months to make this surprise possible. I wish I could express the joy we felt in seeing our "boys" once again. Now everyone was crying, but what a time of rejoicing we had that evening. Don had often said to me, "I guess the next time I see my boys, it will be in heaven," but there they stood that night. I can tell you that the two weeks those men spent with us were the happiest time for Don in those nine years in the States before he went home to heaven. I can never thank our pastor and the church enough for that precious night.

36

THIS WAS NOT A SURPRISE TO THE LORD

THE YEAR OF 2004 was an exciting year, but during that year Don had another mini-stroke and lost the hearing in his left ear overnight. Shortly after, he was also diagnosed with glaucoma.

In one of the earlier chapters, I mentioned that whenever we had a new trial come into our lives, Don would say, "This wasn't a surprise to the Lord. He'll get us through this one just like He always has." This was a good thing to know, because during the next year, 2005, several things began to happen. The pressure in Don's eyes was getting to a very dangerous level. The doctor put him on higher doses of eye drops to try and control the pressure. I just prayed that Don wouldn't lose his sight. He had so little that he could really enjoy doing, and one of these was watching old World War II DVDs. Praise God, that although he could no longer read, he could still watch TV. Don was also having some problems with sinus infections, so the doctor put him on a special nose spray. This however, had some serious side effects. The nose spray contained steroids, and Don began to have problems with his diabetes. They changed his nose spray, and then he began to have problems with his blood sugars dropping too low. He would go into a lethargic state where he began to sweat profusely, and his body temperature would drop to dangerous levels. The first time it happened, it took eight hours in the emergency room to bring his body temperature back to normal. Don never remembered these episodes, but they were terrifying to our family.

It would take a few days to get his strength back after each time this happened, and then we would just continue going to therapy, eating out, and going to church as much as possible. During this same period of time, Don was having some real problems with his breathing at night, and it seemed that he was getting more and more confused. The doctor ordered a sleep apnea study. The results showed that every few minutes, he would literally stop breathing for two minutes at a time. We left the hospital the next morning at 6:00 a.m. Don was very disoriented, and when he drove his power chair up the ramp into our minivan, he forgot to bend his head forward. (He had to do this each time, because the entrance was just a couple centimeters lower than it should have been for him.) He bumped his head hard, and the fusion in his neck acted as a lever to break his neck again. We went back to the hospital, and they did x-rays, an MRI, and a CT scan. This time the T-1, T-2, and T-3 vertebrae were broken. Don had to go through another surgery where surgeons placed two rods from the bottom of the first fusion at C-7 down to the T-4 vertebrae and ten screws down his back. They then took a piece of bone out of his hip and fused it in that area. He had to wear a neck brace for several months. This surgery was another very difficult time for him, because he was in such pain.

While in the hospital, they fitted him with a CPAP machine to help him breathe better at night and therefore sleep better. When he was discharged, they immediately began home health therapy until he was strong enough to go out for therapy once again. He seemed to be bouncing back a little quicker this time. The speech therapist did an evaluation test to see where he was in his understanding and word-finding. The last evaluation had been done about two months before he broke his neck again, and it had taken three sessions of one hour each time to complete the test. This time he completed the test in one session of only forty-five minutes. The CPAP machine had literally brought back the function of his brain. It had been so deprived of oxygen with the sleep apnea that it was impossible for it to function correctly. We were amazed. All of sudden he began to talk with more clarity and was finding the words easier. He was very happy. He began to really enjoy listening to preaching more, because he could understand the messages.

Pastor DeMichele told Don that whenever he felt as if he was ready to preach a message, he would be happy to turn the service over to him. Finally, Don said he would try. He had me look up one of his messages that he preached years before, and he studied it for several days and even had the speech therapist go over the message with him. The Sunday night he preached the message, I could tell that he was really becoming confused about some of the things that he was saying. He tried to stick with reading the message, but he would get lost. I knew he was not happy about the way it went. Pastor DeMichele told him that whenever he was ready to preach again to let him know, but that night was the very last message Don ever preached.

I honestly had not understood all that Don lost with the stroke. I asked him several times why he didn't want to preach again. He would not answer me. As I have said many times, he never complained about anything. He just praised God for His goodness. The kids and I had always gone to Don with any questions we had concerning the Bible. I knew that after the stroke, he would always tell them to ask me about it. I thought it was because of his difficulty in finding the right words. That was not it at all. One day he said, "Honey, please tell the kids not to come to me with their questions anymore, because I do not know the answers." I knew that he had had to learn the books of the Bible again, but I thought it was just part of putting everything in his mind back in order. However, that morning he started crying and said, "The one thing I can't understand is why my knowledge of the scriptures was taken away from me." My heart broke for him. Don loved the Word of God and loved studying it. He'd had such an understanding and knowledge of the scriptures before the stroke that it had always amazed me. No matter what question someone would ask, Don could take him right to the scripture. Now it was just an empty void. He didn't seem to have a resource to draw from when someone asked him a question. However, he seemed to understand the preaching of God's Word and enjoyed it. Sometimes he even would disagree with something he felt was being presented wrong, but to reason this out in his own mind, he couldn't do it. It really was a strange phenomenon. He may have had limited knowledge of the scriptures now, but it didn't keep him from witnessing. He had not lost his love for bringing souls to Christ.

A really fun time with our whole family.

37

THE SUFFERINGS OF THIS PRESENT TIME

Romans 8:18: "For I reckon that the sufferings of this present time are not worthy to be compared with the glory which shall be revealed in us."

THE YEAR 2006 started with a small surprise in January: Don bumped his head again. Back to the hospital for more x-Rays and a CT scan. We dodged a bullet this time. Although his head and neck hurt and his arms and legs went numb for a while, there wasn't any serious damage done. He had to wear his neck brace for a period of time, but soon the headaches stopped. We really praised the Lord that nothing had been broken or jarred lose this time.

Although Don did not have to return to the hospital that year, he still had to battle infections and pneumonia. He seemed to be getting stronger, though. One thing that Don really loved was taking some of the grandkids to therapy with him. He'd push himself to show the kids how strong he was. They loved it, and so did he.

He enjoyed taking them out to eat once in a while, and they enjoyed it too. We also had a new grandbaby that brought a lot of joy to him each day.

Things were really going good until July 2, 2007. Don would always take a nap after we came home from therapy. Then I would get him up into a Hoyer Lift and take him into the living room to sit in his recliner for a couple of hours. Getting him into the recliner was quite an ordeal. The lift would not get him very close to the back of the seat in the recliner, but we worked out a way to get him back far enough to be comfortable. But, in doing this, the straps of the Hoyer lift would sometimes come loose. I almost always checked them before getting him out of the recliner and back into bed, but for some reason I didn't check them one evening. They looked like they were hooked correctly, but when I started raising up the lift, one of the straps came loose. Don was already swinging away from the chair when the strap came undone. It literally dumped him out on the wooden floor. He screamed out in pain, and I knew as soon as I heard that, he was badly injured. We had medical alert pendants that were usually nearby, but somehow I had forgotten to put one back on his tray, and I didn't have mine either. I was terrified, because I knew if I let go of him to reach a phone, I would be putting him in a position that would put his whole weight on his injured leg. I tried to hold him and get the strap back in place, but every movement was excruciating to him. I finally had to slowly lower the lift and leave him there on the floor so I could call 911. Praise the Lord they came within a very short time. They gently examined Don and knew he had some serious injuries. They put him on a gurney as carefully as they could and rushed him to the hospital.

His injuries were worse than I had imagined. His hip was completely crushed, and his leg was broken. Even though he'd fallen only about a foot, his bones were so thin and fragile they easily broke. At the time Don was still on blood thinners, but somehow the doctor did not see this on his chart. They took him straight to surgery and operated on his hip to try and repair all the damage that was done. It took several hours.

That night I noticed that his bandages were soaked with blood, so I called the nurse. She said that it wasn't too unusual for that to happen and the doctors had left orders not to change or remove his bandages until he came the next day. The next morning the nurses were very concerned with the amount of blood on the bandages and also on the sheets. They took his blood pressure and also did several blood tests on him. The results showed that he had lost so much blood that he was in very serious danger. They started blood transfusions, but his blood pressure still would not increase. His doctor came in and took off the dressing. He could not believe how much blood Don had lost. I asked him if it could be from the blood thinners he was on at the time of the surgery. The doctor looked shocked and said, "He was on blood thinners? How could that have gotten past us?" He immediately had a PICC line put into Don's arm and started giving him platelets along with the blood. It took two days before the bleeding actually slowed down and they could get his blood levels back up to a safe place.

However, there was another problem. In all of the worry about losing so much blood, they hadn't even addressed the problem with his broken leg. Don kept telling them that it really hurt whenever they moved him, but they thought it was from the broken hip. This may sound like I'm making all of this up, but this is exactly what he went through. I asked one of the nurses when they were going to set his leg, and her answer was that she had no idea what I was talking about. I decided I was not going to let him lay there and suffer, so I went home and brought back a boot that had been used for transferring him in therapy before, when his leg had been broken previously. I put the boot on him, and it immediately relieved some of the pain. The next day the doctor came in, and I asked him why they hadn't done something before about his leg, but he just didn't think it was that important.

When they discharged him, he was once again on home therapy. This time it took two months before he was healed enough to go back to outpatient therapy. He was really glad to be able to go out of the house again, but his recuperation proved hard, long, and very difficult. I had always tried to take care of Don in a way that was the least stressful and painful for him, but now it was more difficult than ever. Praise God for my son and grandson, who were there many times to help me. Don was fitted with a leg brace to wear anytime he was out of bed. This helped a great deal, but his therapist, Barb, and I were always afraid of breaking that leg again when transferring him.

After getting over this last battle, he did pretty well for several months. We were able to go out to therapy, to eat, and to church. He was really happy and just beamed when we were at church with all of our family gathered around us. Things were looking good. Then, in March 2008, he was back in the hospital with the flu. He'd become very dehydrated and weak. This time he was in the hospital for only two days. Then he began to suffer from bladder infections. It just seemed as if nothing would clear it them up. When he became very sick and in tremendous pain, we knew that something was really wrong. His doctors put him back into the hospital to do a biopsy. When the doctor came out to tell us what they had found, we knew by the look on her face that it was not going to be good news.

38

OUR LAST JOURNEY TOGETHER: A JOURNAL OF OUR TIME TOGETHER DURING THE LAST YEAR OF DON'S LIFE

It's November 2008, and as I sit here in the hospital by Don's bed, I know we are heading toward the end of our journey together. What an incredible journey it's been. I wish every woman could experience the love and companionship that I have had the privilege of sharing with a man who has always made me feel wanted and needed and cherished. He is a man who has loved me through "thick and thin." To him I was always beautiful, no matter what size I happened to fit into at the time. One time he was teasing me and said, "You know that someday your clothes are going to have a nervous breakdown, because they never know on what size they will fit." It was in the "thin" times that he made this observation.

Oh, did I mention he was also very wise? He knew just when the right time was to say something like that!

The doctors told us yesterday that Don has bladder cancer. This was not something we ever expected hear. When they told Don, he said, "I always wondered how I would feel if someone said that I had cancer. Well, I have cancer! We'll deal with it just like we have dealt with other trials. This one's not a surprise to the Lord either." They presented a treatment plan, but it sounds very difficult with all the other physical problems Don has. The decision will have to be up to him. I, of course, would want him to do whatever it would take to keep him here longer, but this doesn't sound like it has a lot of hope of giving him much longer to live, and he would be very sick for weeks at a time.

It's just a week until Thanksgiving, and we are not sure if Don will be out of the hospital by then or not. I always stay in the hospital with him to help with his care and mostly just to be with him. I've done that for many years now, so one way or another, we will have Thanksgiving together. It seems like we have actually spent several Thanksgivings in the hospital. It may not be the preferred place to have Thanksgiving dinner, but somehow that doesn't seem very important right now. Luis Yañez called us a few days ago to tell us that the church in San Rafael wanted to have us listen by phone to the anniversary service this coming Sunday. He told us that it would be a special one. I was telling one of the nurses about it and thought that we would have to miss out on that service. But she said, "Somehow we will make this possible if you can call Mr. Yañez and give him the number of the phone in this room." I told her that I would do that.

It's Sunday, November 23, 2008, and God gave us a very special blessing this morning starting at six o'clock. It was ten o'clock in Argentina. The nurse brought in a conference phone and set it up in our room, and we had the privilege of listening to the special thirty-fourth anniversary service that was dedicated entirely to us. When I called Luis a couple of days ago to give him the room phone number, I told him about the cancer. We cried together and prayed that the Lord would be glorified through all of this. The anniversary service was not only dedicated to us, but every song they sang had been one of Don's favorite songs when we were there. One of Don's favorite ministries was the children's choir. They sang the songs they knew that he had really enjoyed, and a dear little Korean lady in the church sang "God Will Take Care of You" in Korean, and our choir director sang the verses in Spanish. There were wonderful testimonies, thanking us for having brought the Gospel to San Rafael, and the message was a tremendous encouragement to both of us. All of this service had been planned before they had any idea that Don would be in the hospital diagnosed with terminal cancer. God certainly knew our needs this morning, and He so graciously gave us a blessing that we had not expected.

Don was in the hospital for over a week, but now he's feeling much better. The painful spasms that he was having have pretty much diminished. He's had some time to think about the treatment plan and has decided against it. Talk about mixed emotions! I'm relieved that he won't have that terrible nausea and flu-like symptoms for weeks and weeks, but my heart feels so heavy at the thought of losing him soon.

It's February 2009, and for the past three months, we have actually put the cancer on the back burner. Life has gone on as usual. Don has felt pretty good, and we have continued to go to his physical therapy twice a week. One of the things that Don has always enjoyed is going out to eat after his therapy sessions. It's one of the few things we can do together that just seems like a normal thing to do. We are never in a hurry to finish eating, and we have enjoyed each other more than ever.

Don never complains about anything, so I never know if he is hurting or not except for the pained look on his face sometimes. We've had some emotional setbacks this past month, but we know that the Lord is able to help us through these valleys, as He always has.

It's March, and Don has started having blood clots again that cause terrible spasms, and he's back in the hospital now. It's so hard to see him suffer, and the bladder spasms get worse and worse. The picture that the doctor paints isn't a pretty one, but Don just smiles and says, "I'll be with the Lord soon." A couple of nights ago, we were praying, and he said, "Lord, I certainly have nothing to complain about." I thought, here is this wonderful man lying in bed with so many physical problems and experiencing horrible pain, and he has nothing to complain about. In all of these years, he has never complained about having to lay in his bed a great deal of the time waiting for me to take care of every physical need that he has. I honestly can't imagine how that would feel. Sometimes at night I'll lay there in the dark and try to be very still and just imagine what it would be like to not be able to move my body to be more comfortable. The one thing about his paralysis is that he still feels the pain when his body is in one position too long. During the night he sometimes moans in his sleep, and I know it's because he's hurting. I get up and try to get him into a more comfortable position. But he still doesn't complain about it, and often feels bad, because I had to get up and take care of him.

It's April, and Don was in the hospital for three weeks this time. They thought it would be an overnight stay, and he has suffered more than you can imagine. He's had to have three transfusions and had a reaction to the last one. They still are not sure whether he had a heart attack or not, but they cannot give him anymore transfusions for fear of a worse reaction. He is extremely anemic. They talked to us about sending Don home under a new system that is called "bridging." We have a nurse, a doctor, and someone to help bathe him and also to do some physical therapy. They all come to the house. It is set up to help us between the hospital stay and hospice. I'm so grateful for them and for their help.

It's now November 2009—nearly a year that we've been on this last journey together. Don is so ready to go home to be with the Lord. His pain increases with each new day, but his spirit doesn't diminish with the pain. We went on hospice in May, and they gave him a couple of months at most to live. But they didn't know my Don, the fighter, the one who never would give up. He stayed in physical therapy for nearly fifteen years, always trying to get stronger and improve his mobility. He has enjoyed working and kidding around with the therapists. He is so grateful for the tremendous job that they have done through the years, especially Barb, who worked with him for over seven years. They all love Don in return.

He's become a favorite with his hospice nurse, Brook, and Kennett, the hospice social worker. During these months we have all laughed together, cried together, and have continued to be amazed at our "Energizer Bunny." He is well known in their meetings for his sweet attitude and his uncomplaining spirit. He loves to make them laugh, and they always feel better when they leave than when they came. They have become part of our family. There is one dear man who volunteers to come and sit with Don for two hours each week. During this time I usually do grocery shopping or run other errands. When I returned after the first visit, I was surprised to see Don still sitting up in bed talking after two hours. He looked exhausted, but what surprised me most was that he was sitting there with his Bible on his bed table in front of him, and the volunteer had another one that he was using. I knew that one of those Bibles had not been in the room when I left. After Don's stroke he had a very difficult time trying to remember scriptures and where they were found in the Bible. But it didn't stop him from witnessing. On this first visit with the volunteer, he started witnessing to him. Since he could not quote the verses, Don had the man go out into the garage and get one of his old Bibles off the bookshelf out there. He would have the man look up one of the words in the verse in the concordance in the back of the Bible and read it out loud. They did this for the whole two hours. When I got there, Don was literally exhausted from trying to think and talk for those two hours. He witnessed to the volunteer every week for a couple of months. He loves this man and wants so much to see him come to know Christ as his Savior. Don has become too weak to talk very much, and it is very hard for him to find the words he wants to say. That dear man told me that he has missed those talks the last few weeks, but I believe he will never forget them. Above everything else, Don loves souls and has never stopped trying to win someone to Christ.

These past few weeks have been precious as we knew the time was growing short. I finally learned the game of football. I no longer come in to just watch the touchdowns, but now I watch and enjoy the whole game with him. We spent a lot of time this past year laughing, crying, and praying together. Don has always been a night owl, but these late hours when I'm getting him ready to go to sleep have become our favorite time together. We are actually together nearly 24/7, but these hours have been very special. The very last thing we do every night since our first date is pray together. His prayers have become shorter and shorter as he grows weaker, but he always manages to pray, "God, please take care of my wife." I will always be grateful that we had this year to prepare for his home going and the precious memories that we have shared together.

Friends come to visit him, and they always leave smiling. Don just has a way of encouraging people and making them comfortable around him, joking with them and kidding with them if he knows they will give it back to him. We've had pastor and missionary friends who came to visit him the last couple of months, and he has been so happy to be with them. He always loved being with his preacher friends.

One of the great joys has been the calls from our national pastors, "his boys," as he so lovingly calls them, and also from our church people in San Rafael. They have ministered to us during this whole difficult year, encouraging us, thanking us, loving us, and including us in many of the services by way of conference calls and over the Internet. What a blessed, joyful time it has been. I can never thank the Lord enough for being there, present with us every moment.

In late September one of our national pastors told us that his church was outgrowing its facilities. When he hung up, Don said, "Honey, get the pastor's directory and our list of supporting pastors. We are going to raise the money to build a new building for them." He was already very weak, but we worked out a plan to try and raise the money. I would call and get our pastors on the phone, and then Don would try and talk to them to let them know how much he appreciated what they'd done for Argentina and for us. He would then ask if his wife could explain about a need that we had. God wonderfully blessed. He has been able to raise most of the funds for this project. There are going to be thousands of souls saved in this new building. I believe that God gave this work for Don to do at the end of his life to bring him great joy in being "back in the battle again." I can never thank the Lord enough for doing this. And I want to thank our wonderful supporting pastors for responding so willingly to this need.

Don is growing weaker with each new day. A few days ago, one of our missionary friends called, and he asked Don how he was doing. Don said, very seriously, "Not so good, I'm having a hard time getting out of this place." Don still hasn't lost his wonderful sense of humor.

❦

It's Thursday, November 19, and Don has really perked up some. He asked me for some French toast for breakfast, and we have had a wonderful time talking and watching some sports news on TV. It's amazing how clearly he is talking and thinking today. Last night he wanted me to take him into the living room so he could watch a football game on the larger TV. It was the first time he has been out of bed in three days. He's excited about Shelley getting here today from Kansas. He told her he was waiting for her. We are also expecting Brother Steve Bender, our associate mission director and his wife, Janelle. They are here in the area for a mission conference and wanted to come by for a visit. I know that Don will be going home very soon, and I'm praying for God's grace.

Thursday afternoon, after visiting with Brother Bender and his wife, Don went into a deep sleep from which he never fully woke up. He slept peacefully until Saturday evening, when he began to suffer again from bladder spasms. The hospice nurses came and tried to make him as comfortable as possible, but the spasms continued. My heart cried out to God to just take him home. Hadn't he suffered enough? I sat by his bed and held his hand and tried to comfort him as each pain hit him. About two o'clock Sunday morning, he opened his eyes and looked at me and said, "I love you." If Anna and Shelley had not been there to hear it, I probably would have thought that I imagined it. It was the last thing he said to me. I'll always praise God for that moment.

He continued to suffer through Sunday until about 6:00 p.m. when he finally went into a deep, peaceful coma. From that point on, he didn't seem to be in pain anymore, but his body, which fought for so long, just wouldn't give up. We knew it was just a matter of minutes before he would be going home. Shelley turned on some music by Brother Earl Smith, his favorite singer. Don loved to listen to him and his two favorite songs, "Holy City" and "Because He Lives." As soon as "Because He Lives" finished, Don sighed peacefully, and his body finally stopped fighting the battle.

On the twenty-third of November, 2009, at 4:54 a.m., my husband went home to be with the Lord. At that very moment, he won the battle against pain he had suffered for twenty-eight years. He won the battle against paralysis from his spinal cord injuries. He won a twenty-five-year battle with diabetes and epilepsy, an eight-and-a-half year battle trying to recover from a massive stroke, a four-year-battle with glaucoma, and his final battle against unbearable pain and suffering from bladder cancer. He did not lose any of these battles. He won VICTORY over them when he stepped out of that broken body into the arms of his Savior whom he loved and served faithfully for forty-eight years. Don never lost his love for souls, for missions, or for our fellowship that sent us out as missionaries. He loved and appreciated our pastors for supporting us so generously, giving us the funds to fight the good fight of faith for souls and to reap the harvest.

I had the privilege of being loved by this man in a way that most women just dream about. No, he wasn't Superman. He was just a man totally committed to Christ who loved his Lord, his family, and souls to the very end of his life. Thank you, my precious husband, for a love that saved me from a very probable life of self-destruction and misery. Instead, I had the privilege of a forty-five-and-a-half year, unforgettable journey with this man of God, a man who just wouldn't quit.

39

MEMORIAL SERVICE FOR DON

DON DID NOT want his funeral to be about him, but he wanted Christ to be lifted up, to be honored and glorified. He didn't want us to celebrate his life but to give others who were not saved the opportunity to hear the Gospel and to have a new life in Christ.

I would like to include part of his obituary that our daughter, Shelley, wrote:

Dad, we will miss you so much. You taught us to never give up, to never stop serving God. Your cheerful attitude, even in the face of pain and death, cheered up those friends and family who came by to cheer you up. Even as you lay dying, you were still serving God by telling doctors, therapists, and hospice workers about Him. Your excitement about getting to go to Heaven, getting to see Jesus, and getting to walk again made your home-going easier to bear, although we feel the loss deeply and feel sorrow for our time away from you. But we know that when our time comes, you will be there to greet us and to welcome us home. Thank you for that assurance. Your influence here on earth will continue in the church and people you loved so dearly in Argentina, in the souls that continue to be saved as your spiritual children strive to reach others for the Christ you served for so long and so well. You can truly say with Paul, "I have fought a good fight, I have finished my course, and I have kept the faith. Henceforth there is laid up for me a crown of righteousness which the Lord, the righteous judge, shall give me at that day; and not to me only, but unto all them also that love his appearing" (II Timothy 4:7-8).

Thank you for the wonderful legacy you have left behind.

We had the privilege of having some of Don's wonderful preacher friends attend his funeral, and they were such a wonderful blessing to our family that day. Pastor John Paisley talked of their friendship that began in Bible College in 1963. He told of Don's love for souls and his non-complaining spirit. Our assistant mission director, Brother Steve Bender, talked about Don's love for Argentina and the work that he did down there. He read some testimonies from other missionaries in Argentina. He told of ways that Don had had an impact on lives of which we never even knew about. Brother Ruben Garcia, assistant pastor of Treasure Valley Baptist Church, talked of his friendship with Don and how he had always left encouraged after visiting Don, whether it was in the hospital, at home, or at church. He told of Don's wonderful attitude to everyone he met and how he would always answer the question, "How are you doing, Brother Don?" with a smile and say, "I'm doing *great!*"

Three things about Don were mentioned by everyone who spoke: his love for souls, how he always encouraged everyone, and how he never complained about the hard things that God had allowed in his life. Then Pastor Rick DeMichele preached a very clear message on salvation. There were many unsaved people who attended the service, and only eternity will tell us if any received Christ or not. I do know the service touched many lives, and several wanted to know why Don always remained so full of joy when going through all he went through. It opened up many opportunities to witness for Christ.

Some of the testimonies read that day are from some of our children and grandchildren.

From our daughter, Donna:

> My memories of my dad are many. Some of my fondest memories are when he was a pastor in Long Beach, California. We always had family devotions in the evenings. We would always joke around and make Dad laugh. Then we would settle down for him to read the Word of God to us. It was always a goal of mine to make him laugh. I loved to hear him preach and the way he would make me and others laugh. His laugh and smile are how I will always remember him.

—— ⊗⊗⊗ ——

From our daughter, Shelley:

> *My Dad, My Hero:* My dad is Don Espinosa. To some that doesn't mean anything, but to me and to hundreds of people around the world, it is the name of a great hero of faith. My dad taught me many things in life, but the most important one is what I want to share with you: *never* stop serving God. As a child and as a teenager, I thought my dad was the strongest man in the world. When I was fourteen, he broke his neck on the mission field in Argentina; he lost his physical strength, but I saw a different kind of strength emerge. He was told he probably wouldn't walk again, but I saw his determination and watched him walk out of the hospital. We returned to the States, where he had a bone fused in his neck, and people told him this would be a good excuse to quit the mission field. He refused. He loved the Argentine people too much for that. Years went by, and he had more surgeries, learned to walk again more

than once, and he always returned to the mission field. There were too many people left who hadn't heard the Good News of Christ. Even when he ended up confined to a wheelchair much of the time, he still kept on serving God. Eight years ago, he suffered a massive stroke and finally had to leave the people he loved so much. But he did not give up. He did not stop serving God. And even with all the pain and suffering, he never lost his cheerful attitude. He always said, "A live dog is better than a dead lion." I must have heard that hundreds of times! And now he has finished his race. Cancer took its toll. But Dad didn't give up. NEVER. Even as he lay there dying, even as his body was ravaged by his cancer that couldn't be beaten, he was still serving God. My mother told me one day he spent two hours witnessing to the hospice worker who came to stay with him. My dad's mind was not clear like it used to be—he couldn't remember the references for verses; he had little strength left, but he didn't give up. And even though he could barely say hello, he spent the last few weeks of his life contacting pastors to try to raise funds for a mission building in Argentina so that more of the people he loved so much could come hear the gospel. I believe he served God with his last breath. To me, that is a true hero. Thank you, Dad.

From our only son, John:

Memories of My Father: I have a lot of wonderful memories of my dad, but the following stand out from the rest. I remember the fishing trips up in Valle Grande in Argentina every year, where we would stay in a tent next to a beautiful stream and walk down to the river and catch trout. My father could walk and fish for hours without catching anything, but he would never give up, and as soon as he caught one, I would run over and fish right next to him, hoping to also catch one. He always knew how to find the holes where the big ones were. He spent many hours getting my line untangled and trying to save his special spinners I would get caught in the rocks. He taught me tricks on now to catch the big ones, and until this day I still use those same tricks. I remember those days when we couldn't wait to see a small hole in one of his T-shirts he was wearing. We would jump on him and shred it to pieces. He would just stand there and laugh. My poor mother had to have a large supply of T-shirts put away for him. I remember the many lunch hours where we would sit around the table after we ate and watch him perform his "many faces" routine and laugh about it for hours. He was always a great entertainer. I can remember getting up early every Sunday morning and going with him several hours before the morning service to pick up people all around town and out of town that had no other means of transportation to get to church. Afterward we would take them back home. He would always take me on trips with him and listen to preaching messages on cassettes for hours, and he would patiently answer all the questions I had about God and the Bible. I remember watching him buy flowers for my mother and write crazy notes to her. He was very romantic and always a gentleman with my mother. That is something I learned from him, and my wife says that is one of the reasons she fell in love with me. He was a real example of how a man should love and treat his wife. I never saw them fight or argue, but just love each other. I remember as a teenager when I was big enough to fit in his clothes and shoes, and when he would get something new, I would say, "Dad, nice shirt!" And he would always say, "Get your juicy eyeballs off of it!" We did that for many years until I eventually outgrew his clothes, at which time I think he was relieved. I can remember my father's love and generosity toward the Argentine people, who he loved so dearly. One of many examples is when Treasure Valley Baptist church gave him a huge love offering to use however he wanted. He took the money and supplied food for fifty-seven families for three years. There are so many more memories that I could tell, but I just want to say, "Dad, I love you. You're the man."

From our daughter, Anna:

I Remember When: I remember as a three-year-old getting up early each Sunday morning and going with my dad in our truck to pick up the people for church. I remember he would sit me right next to him in the truck so I wouldn't fall out. I remember the first time I saw him after we had our car accident. I was seven years old and thought that I would never see him again. It had been three weeks. I remember our camping trips and how when he was done fishing he would sit on the edge of the freezing-cold river with his feet in the water. I remember trips to the dentist when I was too afraid to open my mouth and how he would try to ease my every fear. I remember when my parents brought me back to the States for college and how my heart broke as I watched them drive away. I remember our last camping trip, while I was home for Christmas break, when I was sure some animal (a really large animal) had walked over the top of the truck that my friend and I were sleeping in and I called him to help us. It took him twenty minutes just to get out of his sleeping bag. I remember when I graduated from Bible College and he was there in his wheelchair to hand me my diploma and how we were both crying. I remember when I went back to Argentina to work with him. I remember when he had his stroke, and my mom and I had to wait nearly twenty-four hours to get the results of the test. I remember being next to him in hospital room and wondering if he was going to be OK. I remember when we were in Texas and he was trying to learn to walk again. I remember how he made all of his therapists laugh and how he said his new ministry was among them. I remember when I had my first baby and how I could hear him outside of my room cheering me on. I remember when we found out that he had terminal cancer. He never once complained of the pain he felt. Every time I walked into his room, I'd ask, "How are you feeling, Dad?" He would always smile and say, "Great!"

As a kid and teenager, I dealt with many fears. He would sit with me for a long time, praying and reading Scripture to me. He had me memorize Deuteronomy 31:6: *"Be strong and of a good courage, fear not, nor be afraid of them: for the Lord thy God is with thee, he it is that doth go with thee; he will not fail thee nor forsake thee."* As I sat there next to my mom watching my dad take his final breath, I thought, you know, I have always been afraid of this. As a little girl I would go and get in my parents' bed and cry, because I was terrified that something would happen to my mom and dad, and I would lose one or both of them. So as I sat there waiting for my worst nightmare to come true, God gave me a peace that I cannot explain. I know that he is with the Lord now. He can walk, and talk, and maybe even fish again. He isn't suffering or agonizing anymore. God has been so good to me. He gave me a great dad, someone I could look up to and cherish. Dad, I miss you so much and I love you with all my heart. Thank you for your unconditional love and for teaching me about the Lord Jesus. Thank you for taking me to Argentina and for the thousands of adventures we've had. Thank you for teaching me to work hard and never give up. I'm sure glad God gave me to you to be my dad.

From an essay that our granddaughter, Jessica Espinosa, wrote for school shortly before her grandpa passed away:

These Are the Reasons I Admire Don Espinosa, My Grandpa. A while ago, while my grandpa and his family were in Argentina, they were driving on a street. Their back tire blew up and their car rolled over, which caused my grandpa's broken neck, and this is why my grandpa is paralyzed. I admire my grandpa, because he followed God's will to be a missionary in Argentina. I honor my grandpa, because he is a strong man, even though he has cancer. He never complains or anything, but he will just give you a smile. I esteem my grandpa because he loves God and my family with all of his heart. He is so excited to get to Heaven to see the Lord and his sister, Dolores. Furthermore, I respect my grandpa because he always tells us stories about his life. Sometimes he tells us stories about when he was in the army, when he was in Bible College, and when he served as a missionary in Argentina. Most importantly, I love my grandpa because he has led many people to Christ and started churches in Argentina. In conclusion, if my grandpa and his family had not gone down to Argentina, my mom and her family would not have gotten saved, and my mom wouldn't have met my dad. Even though my grandpa is going to be gone soon, I am happy for what he has done here and the example he has set for everyone.

From our ten-year-old grandson, Diego:

My Grandpa Is My Inspiration: To me, my grandpa is my inspiration because of all the stuff he has been through. It's just amazing. I don't even know how he did it! It's just unbelievable, and all of his preaching and getting people saved and stuff… Grandpa is my hero, and no matter what, he will always be my hero. I will always love you, Grandpa!

———— ⊂∞⊃ ————

From our son-in-law Nathan Daniel:

As a son-in-law who has known Don Espinosa the shortest period of time, and sadly, not during the best years of his life nor ministry, watching him during the last five years of his life has amazed me. In 2004 Anna and I came to see her parents during their mission conference. A great man was given honor as a missionary to Argentina for his faithfulness to God and commitment to winning souls for Christ. I now understood what a great servant he was as the church surprised him with his national pastors coming to the platform to express their love for this man.

A football player is a wimp compared to my father-in-law who showed no sign of pain and no communication that he was in pain. A few thoughts come to mind when I think of this great man of God—pastor, husband, dad, and friend—who now has a mansion in Heaven. I know Heaven will be better for this man who was paralyzed and now can walk. I understand Mark 9:43, 45 clearer now. And I think of Acts 9:16, how he suffered in this life, but according to John 11:4, his sickness was for the glory of the Son of God; for this man we call beloved praised his Savior through it all—as the old hymn says—he learned to trust in God and to depend on His Holy Word.

He fought a good fight, he has kept the faith, and he more than finished his course, raising money in his last days for a new building in Argentina. He has received his crown of righteousness. No greater inheritance can the patriarch of his family leave than knowing he raised godly children who know the Lord as their savior and who look to see his grandchildren come to Christ. This is Don Espinosa's greatest accomplishment. I will miss Dad, who Pastor Rick DeMichele calls with utmost respect "the apostle to Argentina." What a legacy!

———— ∞∞∞ ————

From Pastor Carlos Cejas, one of Don's "preacher boys":

I'm Pastor Cejas from Temple Baptist Church of Bowen, Argentina. I would like to tell you about my experience working with Pastor Espinosa.

I accepted Christ into my heart as my Savior in 1985 at Temple Baptist Church of San Rafael. At that time, I had the privilege to talk to Pastor Espinosa for the first time. I have to tell you that from that moment until this day he left a mark and a deep spiritual imprint in my spiritual life that has helped me serve the Lord until this time in my ministry.

Pastor Espinosa was a great man of God in every aspect of life. When he went to the pulpit to preach, he had everyone's attention because of his enthusiasm, his passion, and of course, his humor. He always had a joke to make us laugh during the message, but that didn't mean that he wasn't biblical, because he was a very biblical man, and he preached and taught what the Bible says.

By God's grace, I had the privilege to work by his side and by his wife's side for some years, in which they taught me a lot of things about the ministry. He was always thinking about the lost souls and how to win them to the Lord. He was a great soul winner. One of his favorite verses was I Corinthians 9:19: "I made myself servant unto all that I might gain the more."

However, Pastor Espinosa didn't just learn the verse, he went out and won as many as he could. He was a man with a tremendous vision. He would see a neighborhood or new place and would take it as a challenge to work there, winning souls from house to house, passing out tracts, and showing the movie *The Burning Hell*. Whatever it took, he always had a burden to win more souls. As a person he had an impeccable testimony. I'm not saying that he was perfect or without any mistakes, but his testimony was one to imitate. He was a man respected, not only by the members of the church, but all over the town of San Rafael. Pastor Espinosa has left a tremendous mark and imprint in that town. They remember him as a man of his word, honest and upright in all his ways. Let me tell you it takes a lot to make the people think that way, but my pastor accomplished it. Dear friends, I could talk about my pastor all day, but the time is limited. However, as a pastor and preacher of the Gospel, it is my desire to do as much as possible as he did, but to try and fill his shoes is more than I would be able to do, and his mantle would be more than I could handle. I'm thankful I have this opportunity to tell one more time what a tremendous blessing and privilege my Savior gave me to allow me to have met and worked by the side of a man like Pastor Espinosa. He will always be my pastor.

———— ❦ ————

From Pastor Dante Garcia, his first convert in Argentina and first "preacher boy":

From the deepest part of my heart, I thank God for Pastor Espinosa and his ministry to us. God used him so that I could accept Christ as my Savior and learn to love the Lord. I don't only feel like my spiritual father left this world, but I feel like a hero of the faith is no longer with us. It is impossible to express so many precious teachings that he gave me through his example—love, attitude, reactions, words, spiritual vision, faithfulness, and obedience to God. My life has been marked by his life. It was under his ministry that God called me into the ministry; one of his spiritual daughters is my wife. During the ministry we were called as missionaries to Malargue. God used him to gather the support needed to purchase our church building, our house, and our vehicles that we use for the furtherance of the Gospel. His life's motto was "to win the more," and by God's grace, he reached that objective, because thousands of souls have been saved because of Pastor Espinosa's preaching and his influence.

⚬⚬⚬

From Pastor Luis Yañez, who is now the pastor of Temple Baptist Church of San Rafael:

Our transformed lives are testimony to the great work done by the Lord through His servant. His work will continue. He fought a good fight as a good soldier of Jesus Christ. He ran the spiritual race like an athlete; he waited patiently for the harvest like a farmer, and today the fruits of his labor are souls eternally grateful for being shown the Gospel. He was obedient to God's call. We will never forget his love for souls, and we will never forget his vision. We thank God for our pastor, Don Espinosa, who despite the problems with the language, did not turn back when he broke his neck in the car accident. Because of his illness, he endured as "seeing the invisible." We thank God that, despite all odds, our pastor "fulfilled" his ministry, leaving us examples of what God can do with a heart willing to obey. We want you to know that the seed planted by this faithful man continues to bear fruit. The testimony left by this man of God continues to impact lives, and though in his last days his body was spent, he was not in any way the picture of a defeated man, but of a conqueror whose last words spoken to our church in his final days were: "Keep preaching, keep preaching!"

EPILOGUE

THE GOOD FIGHT OF FAITH

I am sitting in the airport in Santiago, Chile, waiting to board the plane for Dallas and then on to Boise to return to my home there. I decided on making this trip several months ago after Don went home to be with the Lord. My son and his family were making the trip to celebrate their daughter's fifteenth birthday with her family in San Rafael. I didn't plan to go this soon after Don went home to be with the Lord, because I wasn't sure how I would handle being there without my husband. I didn't want to make the trip by myself this first time back.

Why do I ever doubt the wonderful grace of our Lord? I wasn't sure just what to expect, but the Lord blessed beyond what I could have ever expected.

The four works that began under our ministry have gone forward and started new ministries. They have grown in grace and knowledge of our Lord Jesus Christ. The reception that I received was so warm and welcoming. They showed me so much love. It was so much more than I could have imagined, and it was such a wonderful time. I made this trip to see Don's last wish carried out, and that was to make sure they received the money to build a new building for the work in Bowen, Argentina. The building is going up quickly, and I was so thrilled to see the size and the progress made on it. However, the biggest blessing was to see the happiness of the people in that church. They have a good variety of ages and family dynamics in the work. This work began because an elderly Russian couple had a desire to see a Bible-teaching church established there. They had been members of another church for many years, but the charismatic movement had taken it over. For over two years, this couple had no one to have Bible study with or anyone with whom they could fellowship. They had had some family members who were saved in San Rafael. The older couple came to meet with the pastors there with the desire to see if someone would be willing to come to Bowen and hold a Bible study. The pastor, Luis Yañez, and associate pastor, Carlos Cejas, began taking turns Sunday afternoons to go and teach, preach, and visit there. Souls immediately began to be saved, and after a few months, Pastor Carlos felt that God was calling him to go and pastor there full-time. He sold his home in San Rafael and invested it all in an old house with a storefront and a lot behind it. The ministry began to grow, and soon this storefront building filled up. God has richly blessed the sacrifices that Pastor Carlos made for the ministry there. Soon they will have a beautiful new facility where they will have room to really grow. What a blessing to see these works going on and souls continuing to be saved.

God was so good to us to let us have a part in taking the Gospel to these precious people. Don truly fought the good fight, he finished his course, and he kept the faith. Only God knows how many souls were saved during his ministry and the number of souls that will continue to be saved until the Lord comes back to take us all home. TO GOD BE THE HONOR AND GLORY.

Update: In February 2012 I had the privilege of returning to Argentina for the dedication of the beautiful new building in Bowen. It was a tremendous blessing to see Don's last effort and desire to see more souls won to Christ in Argentina come to be realized. God continues to bless the churches that He allowed us the opportunity to have a part in starting. It's my hope and desire to see them continue on faithfully until the Lord returns.